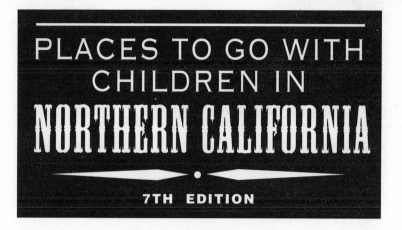

PLACES TO GO WITH CHILDREN IN
NORTHERN CALIFORNIA

7TH EDITION

ELIZABETH POMADA

CHRONICLE BOOKS
SAN FRANCISCO

Library of Congress Cataloging-in-Publication Data
Pomada, Elizabeth.
    Places to go with children in northern California / by Elizabeth
Pomada.
        p.   cm.
    ISBN 0-8118-0261-2 (pb)
    1. California, Northern—Guidebooks. 2. Children—Travel—
California, Northern—Guidebooks. 3. Family recreation—California,
Northern—Guidebooks.   I. Title
F867.5.P66   1993
917.9404'53—dc20   92-24736
                                                                  CIP

Printed in the United States of America.

Distributed in Canada by Raincoast Books
112 East Third Avenue
Vancouver, B.C. V5T 1C8

10 9 8 7 6 5 4 3 2 1

Chronicle Books
275 Fifth Street
San Francisco, CA 94103

CONTENTS

Needless to say, this book was not done by just one person. I must say "thank you" to Lauren and Jennifer, Elizabeth and Deborah, Diana and Marc, Eric and Chris, Cindy and Christopher, and Alan, our "test" children. But most of all, thank you to my pal, editor, chauffeur, idea man, hero, and the biggest child of them all—M.F.L.   *E.P.*

After living in New York City for 30 years, Elizabeth Pomada moved to San Francisco. She learned about Northern California by traveling over 4,000 miles of it to write *Places to Go with Children in Northern California*. Her other books include *California Publicity Outlets*, now published as *Metro California Media*. She and her partner, Michael Larsen, have created the Painted Ladies® series: *Painted Ladies: San Francisco's Resplendent Victorians*; *Daughters of Painted Ladies: America's Resplendent Victorians*; *How to Create Your Own Painted Lady*; *Painted Ladies Revisited: San Francisco's Painted Ladies Inside and Out*; *The Painted Ladies' Guide to Victorian California*; *America's Painted Ladies: The Ultimate Guide to Our Resplendent Victorians*; and the *Painted Ladies Calendars*. They also run the oldest literary agency in San Francisco.

A WORD BEFORE YOU GO

Here, bigger and we hope better than ever, is the seventh edition of *Places to Go with Children in Northern California*. The countryside is as gorgeous and varied as ever, and it was a pleasure exploring again, both to check on places already in the book and to find new discoveries to share with you.

Maybe it's just provincial pride, but we think that the ocean, rivers, trees, sunshine, mountains, all of the breathtaking beauty and richness that Northern California has been blessed with, make it one of the most beautiful areas on earth. More remarkable still is that so much of it has been protected or left in its natural state for us to marvel at.

We were pleased to find that the interest in preserving the state's colorful historical heritage continues to gain momentum. More museums and historic houses dot the landscape than ever. We believe that if you and your children can learn something and have fun at the same time, then the good time is worth twice as much. Most of the places listed here are enjoyable no matter how old you are.

Practically all of the places in *Places* have wheelchair access—indicated with a "W" at the end of the entries—and almost all of the attractions with educational value present special tours for school and other groups.

Most of the nonprofit institutions have gift shops, the sales from which help to sustain museums and nature centers. If you are pleased with what you see, these shops are one way of showing your support.

Most of the nonprofit attractions are staffed largely by volunteers. If you live in the area, another way of showing your support and making new friends is helping out. Some places even have volunteer programs for children, which will be learning experiences for the kids and might even lead to a career.

The goal of *Places* is to include every attraction and special event in Northern California that children will enjoy. Since we concentrate on places to see rather than things to do, we haven't included activities such as bowling, skateboarding, skiing, shooting pool, skating, or miniature golf. So if we do mention a waterslide or balloon site in one area and that sounds like a good destination to you, check the local Yellow Pages to see if there's one nearby. One adventure may lead to another.

We hope that you will help to make the next edition even better. Please write to me at 1029 Jones Street, San Francisco 94109, or call me at (415) 673-0939 if you find an attraction that should be in the next edition, or if you think of a way to make *Places* more helpful to parents and teachers. This edition has benefited from the many people who have contacted us.

We will be happy to send an autographed copy of the new edition to the first person to suggest a new place to visit or one we have overlooked.

If you have any unusual experiences, good or bad, at the places in the book, we would like to know about them. Also, if your children or students write anything memorable about the places they visit, we'd like to see it—and perhaps quote them in the next edition. We would like to make *Places* a dialogue so that it will continue to improve. Many of the places included sent copies of letters that youngsters had written to them, and we've quoted them when it's seemed appropriate. After all, a book for children should have input from children!

Prices do go up and schedules do change, especially in winter and on holidays, so if you're going far, call for up-to-the-minute information and driving and lodging tips. Most places are closed on Thanksgiving, Christmas, and New Year's Day. Local Chambers of Commerce, tourist offices, and the American Automobile Association will also help you plan your trip. And don't forget to stock the car with travel snacks and games, books and books on tape, tissues, wet wipes, and a lot of good humor.

We hope that you will enjoy *Places* and the places it inspires you to visit. Bon voyage!

NORTHERN CALIFORNIA'S TOP 11 PLACES

1. Monterey Aquarium
2. San Francisco Exploratorium
3. Yosemite National Park
4. Oakland Museum
5. Marine World Africa USA, Vallejo
6. Santa Cruz Boardwalk
7. Lawrence Hall of Science, Berkeley
8. San Francisco Zoo
9. California State Railroad Museum, Old Sacramento
10. Point Reyes National Seashore
11. Ardenwood Historic Farm, Fremont

To which I add my personal favorites:
1. John Muir House, Martinez
2. Columbia State Historic Park
3. San Juan Bautista State Historic Park
4. Winchester Mystery House, San Jose
5. Rosicrucian Museum, San Jose
6. Zalud House, Porterville
7. Jack London State Historic Park, Glen Ellen
8. Lachryma Montis, General Vallejo's Home, Sonoma State Historic Park
9. San Francisco Historic Ships at Hyde Street Pier

SAN FRANCISCO

San Francisco has been called a peninsula bounded on three sides by water and one side by reality. What makes the City special? It's both large and small. At about 750,000 people, it's small for a major city. Yet it has the amenities of any great city: opera, ballet, theater, a symphony, shopping galore, and restaurants that will please any palate.

San Francisco is a unique blend of elements:

◆ a beautiful natural setting
◆ cool, fair weather
◆ a history that makes up in color what it lacks in length
◆ a rich multicultural heritage that makes the City hospitable to new people, ideas, and lifestyles
◆ old and new architecture, with the greatest and most beautiful collection of redwood Victorians in the world
◆ a collection of distinct neighborhoods worth wandering in
◆ a world-class mixture of education, business, culture, and religion that attracts visitors and immigrants from all over the world
◆ a size small enough to walk around in yet large enough to provide kids of all ages with plenty of things to see and do.

Consider transportation. You can see San Francisco by foot, bicycle, moped, car, taxi, bus (single or double decker), cable car (regular or motorized), trolley car, subway, helicopter, ferry, sailboat, and even by blimp!

Hungry? San Francisco provides an excellent opportunity to expand your children's enjoyment of the world's cuisine. The first ten blocks of Clement Street in the Richmond District offer the most cosmopolitan concentration of delectable food we know of anywhere. Here, you can feast on Chinese food (including dim sum dumplings and Cantonese-, Mandarin-, and Hunan-style cooking), Japanese, Italian, Indonesian, French, Russian, Persian, Vietnamese, Irish, Thai, and health food, and even barbecue and other American food.

San Francisco suffers from the same problems as any metropolis, but the City's size, human-scale architecture (outside of our mini-Manhattan downtown), and sunny weather give urban blights a more benign quality.

The City has a remarkable capacity for self-renewal. Although still largely populated by the poor and the nefarious, the Tenderloin is being revitalized by Vietnamese refugees. Kids are playing in the streets, stores and restaurants have sprouted up, and the area is adding another neighborhood to the City's rich ethnic mix.

Much of the best of what the City has to offer is free. More than one-third of the attractions in this chapter are free. San Francisco is a walker's paradise. Just strolling around Golden Gate Park or the City's neighborhoods—Chinatown, Japantown, the Mission, Noe Valley, Clement Street, Union Street, or anywhere on the the waterfront from Land's End to the Embarcadero—on a sunny, breezy day is delightful. For views, try the free ride on the outside elevator to the Crown Room at the top of the Fairmont Hotel, one of the best free rides in the world. Or stop by Coit Tower on the top of Telegraph Hill. The observation platform at the top is 210 feet high (open daily, 9–4:30).

Unless you hit one of the City's few hot days, the temperature is usually in the low 60s. So the layered look, which enables you to peel off a jacket or sweater if it gets toasty, is always appropriate.

The "Pinkie," the pink section in the Sunday *Chronicle*, will fill you in on special events that are taking place while you are in town.

Whether you live in the City or are just visiting, whether you are young or just young at heart, whether you want cultural enrichment or just plain fun, San Francisco is one of the best places in the world to spend a week or a lifetime. So as they say these days: "Go for it!"

❖ Golden Gate Ferry to Larkspur or Sausalito

Ferry Plaza, San Francisco 94111. Next to the Ferry Building at the foot of Market Street. (415) 332-6600. Ferries leave the City daily. Call for up-to-date prices and schedules. Bicycles OK. Family fares. W.

The Golden Gate Ferry leaves its slip at the foot of Market Street, passes Alcatraz Island, and docks across the bay. The snack bar serves coffee and snacks, and whether it's sunny or foggy the views are wonderful. Bring a camera.

❖ The Sailing Ship Restaurant

Pier 42–44, San Francisco 94107. Berry Street at the Embarcadero. Dinner, Tues.–Sat. Lunch parties. (415) 777-5771.

The *Dolph P. Rempp*, one of the last of the three-masted topsail schooners to ply the Pacific trade, is open for a "seagoing" dinner. While dining on fine continental cuisine you can "pretend sail" on a ship you saw in *Hawaii* or *Mutiny on the Bounty* and see super views of the bay.

❖ Cartoon Art Museum

665 Third Street, San Francisco 94107. (415) 546-3922. Wed.–Fri., 11– 5; Sat. 10–5; and by appt. Adults, $2.50; 12 and under, $1. Parties.

Original art from cartoon strips, ads, comic books, sports and editorial cartoons, and greeting cards are treated as fine art in this happy museum. Here visitors will see work by Charles Schultz, Gahan Wilson, Jim Davis, and dozens of other favorite cartoonists from the past and present. Film and video cartoons are shown as well.

❖ World of Oil

555 Market Street, San Francisco 94105. (415) 894-6697. Mon.–Fri., 8:30–4:30. Group tours by appt. Free. W.

If you've ever wondered how oil is found, produced, transformed into thousands of products, and used for energy, heat, and lubrication, this is the place to come.

Tapes, films, an energy quiz, and interactive displays show junior scientists how oil was obtained and used in the past. Photos, drilling and rigging tools, and models of offshore wells are eye-openers. Three life-size dioramas show the role oil has played in American life. The first service station and the 1910 kitchen have a nostalgic appeal.

❖ The Old U.S. Mint

Fifth and Mission streets, San Francisco 94105. (415) 744-6830. Weekdays, 10–4. Closed on holidays. Tours by appt. Free. W.

The Granite Lady, a half-hour film, shows the history of California and the part the Old Mint has played in it, from the crackling excitement of the Gold Rush to the terror of the 1906 earthquake and fire. Visitors can see tokens, bank notes, walrus and seal skins, and other forms of money, as well as a stack of 128 gold bars and gold nuggets. In the superintendent's office, the clock reads "Time Is Money." Visitors can strike their own souvenir medal on an 1869 coil press during their 90-minute tour.

❖ The Asawa Fountain

Grand Hyatt Hotel, 345 Stockton Street, San Francisco 94108. Between Sutter and Post. Free.

Ruth Asawa, artist and creator of the Mermaid Fountain in Ghirardelli Square, has given the people of San Francisco a one-stop tour of the people and places that make up the City. This fountain, 14 feet in diameter, on the steps of the plaza of the Grand Hyatt on Union Square, was molded in bread dough—the same dough children use for sculpting—and cast in bronze. And the little people, trees, Chinese dragon, Painted Ladies, and school buses demand to be touched. At the bottom of the fountain is the Ferry Building; as you go around it, you'll see Coit Tower, Broadway, Aquatic Park, the Cannery, the zoo, the Mission district—everything laid out in the same general direction as it is in real life. A group of Noe Valley schoolchildren created one of the fountain's 41 plaques, which depicts the children of San Francisco. Your kids will enjoy figuring out which one it is.

➣ Museum of Money of the American West

Bank of California, 400 California Street (downstairs), San Francisco 94104. (415) 765-0400. Mon.–Thurs., 10–4; Fri. until 5. Free.

This small but nicely mounted collection of money and gold provides a glimpse of banking and mining in the Old West. Each coin is a piece of history. Privately minted coins from Utah, Colorado, and California show the kind of money used before the U.S. Mint was set up in San Francisco. Ingots, gold bullion, currency, and early bank drafts are here, along with counterfeit coins and counterfeit detectors. One method of counterfeiting, "the platinum menace," hollowed out coins and filled them with platinum, then worth much less than gold. Is that why an Oregon two-ounce copper-alloy coin reads "In Gold We Trust"?

➣ Wells Fargo History Room

420 Montgomery Street, San Francisco 94104. (415) 396-2619. Weekdays except bank holidays, 9–5. Group guided tours by appt. Free. W.

Ever wanted to bounce along in a stagecoach? Or send a telegraph message? Or rock a gold-panning cradle? The youngsters can relive the romance of the West in this beautifully designed bilevel museum. Here you'll find gold, money, treasure boxes, art, tools, photos, a map of Black Bart's 28 stagecoach robberies, iron doors from a Wells Fargo office in the Gold Country, Pony Express memorabilia, and a rocking Concord Stage Coach with an audio tape of one young man's trip from St. Louis to San Francisco.

➣ Chinatown

A visit to San Francisco would not be complete without a visit to Chinatown, along Grant Avenue from Bush to Broadway and along Stockton Street from Sacramento to Vallejo. For the curious, there are fortune-cookie factories, fish stores, and temples, as well as shops and restaurants.

The **Golden Gate Fortune Cookie Factory** on Ross Alley, between Washington and Jackson, above Grant, sometimes leaves its doors open so you can see the row of tiny griddles revolving under a hose that squirts dough onto each pan. The pans cook the dough on their way to the cookie-maker, who picks up each browned wafer, pushes it onto a spur for the first fold, inserts the paper fortune, presses the final fold, and puts the cookie in a muffin tin to harden. For more than a peek, make an appointment. (Weekdays, 10–noon): (415) 781-3956.

Tin Hou Temple (125 Waverly Place, fourth floor, 10–5 daily) is dedicated to the Queen of Heaven and boasts a ceiling filled with carved wood mythological figures. Just follow the scent of incense up the stairs.

One of our favorite lunchtime meals is *dim sum*, which means "heart's delights." With dim sum, also called Chinese tea or tea lunch, there's always something to entice every palate. Dim sum is simply little bites of good things. A waitress comes around with a cart from which you choose small plates of such delicacies as shrimp rolls, curry cakes, beef dumplings, spareribs, mushroom turnovers, custard pies, or steamed barbecued-pork buns, *bao*. If your choice is on two plates and there are only two of you, ask for a half-order. You pay for the number of dishes chosen. In Chinatown, we recommend the **Golden Dragon** on Washington, between Stockton and Grant. Our two favorite dim sum restaurants are not in Chinatown proper. **Yank Sing**, at 427 Battery near Clay (415 781-1111), has been called the best in the world. And at **Harbor Village**, #4 Embarcadero Center (415 398-8883), you can get a peek at the bay and the Bay Bridge, then shop in the four buildings that make up Embarcadero Center.

Cultural, historical, and artistic exhibitions are presented in **The Chinese Culture Center**, the forum for the Chinese community (750 Kearny, in the Holiday Inn, third floor; 415 986-1822; Tues.–Sat. 10–4; gallery, free).

❖ Chinese Historical Society of America

650 Commercial Street (between Clay and Sacramento), San Francisco 94111. (415) 391-1188. Tues.–Sat., 12–4. Gift shop. Donation.

Chinese societies throughout California have contributed to this small, hidden museum to show how the Chinese have played an important part in California's development. Ceremonial swords, printing blocks, an altar, porcelain pillows, clothes worn by 19th-century laborers and the high born, opium pipes, photographs, and documents crowd the display space. There are changing exhibits, such as one on the first women to vote in America and another on the first telephone system in San Francisco.

❧ Pacific Heritage Museum
608 Commercial Street (between Montgomery and Kearny), San Francisco 94111. (415) 399-1124. Weekdays, 10–4. Free.

The Bank of Canton has integrated the historic 1875 U.S. Subtreasury Building, once the U.S. Branch Mint, into its architecturally acclaimed world headquarters in San Francisco's Financial District. Exhibits of Pacific Rim culture and history change every 12 to 18 months. During our visit, we were fascinated with "Wings Over the Pacific," which recreated the colorful history of flight throughout the Pacific Rim with hundreds of artifacts, models, engines, and rare photographs.

❧ Cable Car Barn Museum
1201 Mason Street (at Washington Street), San Francisco 94108. (415) 474-1887. Daily, 10–5. Closed holidays. Donation. Museum shop and bookstore.

All three cable car lines in San Francisco are run by the huge revolving red and yellow wheels in the brick cable car barn, built in 1887. Visitors can watch the wheels from a gallery, where there are samples of the cable itself and charts explaining how the cable cars work. You can see scale models, earthquake mementos, old cable car seats, photographs, and the cable cars on display, including the first one to operate in San Francisco, in 1873. An exciting underground viewing room lets you see the cables running under the city streets from the car barn at nine and a half miles an hour. A 16-minute video offers more information.

❧ North Beach Museum
1435 Stockton Street (upstairs in EurekaBank), San Francisco 94133. (415) 391-6210. Mon.–Fri, 9–4. Tours by appt. Free.

Photographs and artifacts in changing thematic exhibits celebrate the City's, and especially North Beach's, colorful past, from the Gold Rush to the 1906 earthquake and fire, to the growth of the neighborhood as the center of the City's Italian community, to the Beat Generation.

❧ Society of California Pioneers
456 McAllister Street, San Francisco 94102. (415) 861-5278. Mon.–Fri., 10–4. Groups by appt. Free. W.

"Thank you for the wonderful exhibit. It was very interesting and long. The dresses on the mannikins were really fancy. I liked how the people advertise their things, like the Ghirardelli Cocoa factory.... I'm glad I wasn't born in those days, because if I'm an adult I would have to skin my knuckles on the washboard when I am washing my clothes. The movies were good and the stories you told were exciting...." So wrote Rebecca, Argonne Elementary School.

The Children's History Gallery has been designed to enhance and augment the fourth-grade California history curriculum. The exhibits reflect the cultural diversity of California's pioneers and emphasize the Hispanic and Gold Rush periods with tools, utensils of daily life, clothing, toys, musical instruments—and two original videos. A scale model of a Wells Fargo Concord stagecoach is displayed in the rotunda. Major San Francisco events of the 1906 earthquake and fire and the 1915 Panama-Pacific International Exposition are recognized with a display of photographs and artifacts.

❖ San Francisco Museum of Modern Art

War Memorial Veterans Building, 401 Van Ness Avenue (at McAllister), San Francisco 94102. (415) 863-8800. Tues.–Fri., 10–5; Thurs., until 9; weekends, 11–5. Adults, $3.50; under 16, $1.50. (Free on first Tues. of each month, 10–5. Reduced rates Thurs. after 5 and for groups.) W.

The museum of modern art offers constantly changing exhibits of paintings, sculpture, works of art on paper, and photography. Ceramics and graphics are part of the permanent art collection—which emphasizes modern masters such as San Franciscans Wayne Thiebaud and Clyfford Still. There are many who feel that children are best able to view modern art, because they're open to everything with no preconceived ideas about what art should be. While looking at a roomful of Jonathan Borofsky's *Chattering Men*, we were inclined to agree.

❖ The Hard Rock Cafe

1699 Van Ness Avenue (at Sacramento), San Francisco 94109. (415) 885-1699. Daily, 11:30–11:30; Fri. and Sat. until 12:30. Reservations for lunch only. Valet parking on Sacramento. Gift shop. W.

The Hard Rock Cafe is just as much a rock-and-roll shrine as it is a restaurant. It's a mecca for rock fans of all ages. Sounds of the great rockers greet you as you walk into a large, two-level room, the walls of which are covered with posters, gold and platinum records, and the guitars of rock stars. The room has a California openness punctuated by a dodge'em car, a motorcycle, and a standard Hard Rock fixture: half of a Cadillac over the entranceway. The menu's California touches lighten the load of affordable golden oldies like ribs, fries, hamburgers, shakes, and banana splits. Expect a wait most of the time. Justin wrote, "My favorite restaurant is Hard Rock Cafe. Why I like this particular place so much is because of the food and what there is to look at. While I'm waiting for my food I can just look around and keep myself entertained. I also like the pinball games they have there....They also play loud rock and roll music which you can sit in your comfortable seats and listen...Hard Rock Cafe is a great and fun place to eat."

❖ Ghirardelli Chocolate Manufactory

Ghirardelli Square, 900 North Point (at Polk), San Francisco 94109. (415) 771-4903. Daily, 11:30–10; later in summer. Parties: 474-3938. W.

Since the beginning of the century, Ghirardelli Stoneground Chocolate has been a popular trade name throughout the West. This red brick, aromatic ice cream and candy shop invokes that name in a nostalgic corner of the old Ghirardelli factory. After filling out an order form and paying the cashier, you claim a table, then take turns watching the chocolate-making machinery in the back of the room until your order number is called. We always dream of diving into the big vats where the chocolate is conched after the beans are roasted, cracked, husked, ground, and mixed with other ingredients. Instead, we dive into a hot fudge sundae, or a delicious extravaganza like the Emperor Norton, with bananas, or the Chocolate Decadence. Or we could opt for a soda or cone.

The square itself is three stories full of stores and restaurants, many with great views of the bay. Here you can find shoes, popcorn, cookies, crafts, books, perfume, clothes, and gifts galore. Jugglers and street entertainers perform on weekends and in summer, free.

❖ Museum of the City of San Francisco

The Cannery, 2801 Leavenworth, San Francisco 94109. Third level, Beach Street and Leavenworth. (415) 928-0289. Wed.–Sun., 11–4. Donation. W.

San Francisco treasures capture the imagination in this glistening museum space. The Disaster Room focuses on the earthquake and fire of 1906 and the earthquake of 1989. Photographs and memorabilia such as dishes and letters that survived line the walls and are featured in free-standing displays. The buggy that transported the fire chief to the hospital during the 1906 quake is a favorite—as is the supersize head of the Goddess of Progress, which crowned City Hall before 1906. The hand-carved wooden ceiling is from a 13th-century Spanish palace purchased by William Randolph Hearst. The Fun Room highlights high times in the City, from Barbary Coast times to the Victorian era to the Summer of Love.

Those who remember the Summer of Love happily will want to run downstairs to the **Best Comics & Rock Art Gallery** on the ground floor (771-9247) for a look at an astonishing collection of handbills, original rock art and posters, toys, collectibles, and comics. There you'll find fabulous posters from Fillmore West as well as rare and new *Star Trek*, *MAD*, and *Little Orphan Annie* comics, trading cards, and books.

Naturally, since the Cannery is a shopping complex, there are many gift and crafts stores and restaurants to browse through. Spectacular views from the third-floor walkway extend from the Golden Gate Bridge to the Berkeley hills.

☆ National Maritime Museum at San Francisco (San Francisco Maritime National Historic Park)

900 Beach Street (at the foot of Polk Street), San Francisco 94109. (415) 556-8177/556-1659. Daily, 10–5; until 6 in summer. Call for calendar of events. Free. W.

The Maritime Museum is a mecca for ship lovers of all ages. The maritime history of San Francisco lives on here in models of clippers, British ships, iron ships, schooners, barkentines, cutters, and cod fishers; and in photos, figureheads, tools, scrimshaw, guns and harpoons, diaries, and ships' logs. The 19-foot sloop *Mermaid*, which one man sailed from Osaka to San Francisco, is on the veranda. Models of the *Queen Mary* along with cargo and warships from World War I to the present are in the steamship room.

☆ San Francisco Historic Ships at Hyde Street Pier (San Francisco Maritime National Historic Park)

Hyde Street Pier (at Aquatic Park), San Francisco 94109. (415) 556-6435. Daily, 10–5, later in summer. Tours & Environmental Living Programs by appt. Adults, $3; ages 12–17 and over 61, $1; under 12, free. W (limited).

The Balclutha, one of the last surviving square-rigged Cape Horners, flies its 25 sails at the Hyde Street Pier. You can spin the wheel, visit the "slop chest" and galley, check out the captain's quarters with its swinging bed, ring bells, and read sea chanties and rousing tales of the Barbary Coast below decks, while the movement of the boat on the water heightens the imagination.

You can also go below decks on the *C. A. Thayer*, a salmon packet, to see the captain's family cabin. There are antique cars waiting for the next docking on the ferryboat *Eureka*. And you can check out the *Alma*, the last remaining San Francisco Bay schooner, or the six-room *Lewis Ark* houseboat. Other boats are docked on occasion, such as the paddle tug *Eppleton Hall* or the steam schooner *Wapama*, and some of these are boardable. On land, there are engine room showings, boat-building classes, movies and videos, and changing exhibits.

⇻ Guinness Museum of World Records

235 Jefferson Street (at Fisherman's Wharf), San Francisco 94133. (415) 771-9890. Sun.–Thurs., 10–10; Fri. and Sat., until midnight. Adults, $6.25; under 12, $3.25. AAA discount. W.

World records from the *Guinness Book of World Records* come to life in this curious museum. You'll be overwhelmed with record-setting objects, audience-participation displays, dramatizations, and multimedia videotapes and films of records being set. You can see the world's tallest man, and the world's smallest book. A collection of the biggest, the smallest, and the mostest.

⇻ Ripley's Believe It Or Not! Museum

175 Jefferson (at Fisherman's Wharf), San Francisco 94133. (415) 771-6188. Sun.–Thurs., 10–10; Fri. and Sat. until midnight. Adults, $6.95; ages 13–17, $5.50; under 12, $4. School tours by appt.

This two-story collection of oddities and puzzles is almost unbelievable. Where else could you see a cable car made from 270,836 matchsticks? The Pietà made of brown paper bags? A stegosaurus made of chrome car bumpers? Here you can walk through an animal kaleidoscope and a rotating tunnel, experience a disasters gallery, and wonder at the man with two pupils in each eye.

⇻ Wax Museum at Fisherman's Wharf

145 Jefferson (at Fisherman's Wharf), San Francisco 94133. (415) 202-0400/885-2023. Daily, 10–10; Fri. and Sat., 9 A.M.–11:30 P.M. Adults, $8.95; seniors & military, $6.95; children, $3.95. Group rates. Parties. One-price tickets available for Wax Museum, Haunted Gold Mine, Medieval Dungeon, and LazerMaze. W. (limited)

Meet Prince Charles and Princess Diana, Abraham Lincoln, Mona Lisa, Michael Jackson, King Tut with his Treasures, Elvis Presley, Peter Pan and Snow White, heroes and villains, in four flights of scenes recreating the past, the present, and the world of the future. The Chamber of Horrors on the lower level is "not recommended for cowards, sissys, and yellerbellies."

⇻ LazerMaze

107 Jefferson (at Fisherman's Wharf), San Francisco 94133. (415) 202-0400/474-6349. Same price and time schedule as Wax Museum at Fisherman's Wharf. Group and party rates.

In this world's first walk-in video game, players may select from three skill levels in attempts to increase scores. In the 3-D fantasy, you experience live laser combat against life-size attack robots, and you have seconds to fire your lazerblaster or else!

❯❯ San Francisco Helicopter Tours

P.O. Box 4115, Oakland 94614. Kaiser Air, Hanger #3, Oakland Airport. (800) 400-2404 or (510) 635-4500. Daily, from 7 A.M. to dark. Call for schedules, prices, and reservations.

Complimentary vans provide fliers with transportation from San Francisco hotels or Fisherman's Wharf to the airport, where you'll be whisked aloft for a 20- or 30-minute trip, a trip to the wine country, a twilight flight, or an evening dinner flight. Charters and custom tours are available.

❯❯ USS Pampanito

Pier 45 (near Fisherman's Wharf), San Francisco 94133. (415) 929-0202. Daily, 9–6; until 9 on weekends and in summer. Adults, $4; juniors, $2; children and seniors, $1.

This World War II–vintage submarine is a floating museum and a memorial to the men who served in the "silent service." Self-guided tours through the cramped quarters are explained via audiotape.

❯❯ Alcatraz Island Cruise and Tour (GGNRA)

Pier 41, 94133. (415) 546-2896. Frequent sailings on the Red & White fleet daily. Advance ticket purchase through TICKETRON or by phone with a charge card is strongly suggested. To cruise around the Rock on a Red & White Cruise tour narrated by Frank Heaney, a former prison guard, call the above number. Boats leave Pier 41 regularly. Once docked, you'll walk with the self-guided audio tour available when you purchase your ticket. Call for up-to-date schedules and prices.

Wear walking shoes and bring a sweater on this educational, fascinating-yet-depressing, self-guided walking tour of Alcatraz. One friend calls the two-hour trip a sure-fire way to stop juvenile delinquency. Alcatraz is part of the Golden Gate National Recreation Area, nationally protected park land along the coast.

❯❯ Bay Cruises

On a sunny day in San Francisco, there's nothing nicer for the family than getting out on San Francisco Bay. You can take a ferry that goes to Sausalito, Angel Island, Tiburon, or Marine World, or simply take a guided-tour cruise of the bay, under the Golden Gate and Bay bridges. The **Red & White Fleet** offers a 45-minute cruise and six other choices.

In California, call (800) 445-8880 or (415) 546-2896. Boats leave from Pier 41 and 43 1/2. The **Blue & Gold Fleet**, leaving from Pier 39, has a 1 1/4 hour Bay Cruise. For schedules and prices, call (415) 705-5444. Group rates. W.

❧ The San Francisco Experience

Pier 39, San Francisco 94133. (415) 982-7394. Daily, every half-hour, 10 A.M.–10 P.M. Adults, $6; Ages 6–16 and military, $5. Group rates. School programs. Parties. W.

Seven screens, 32 speakers, 3 movie projectors, and 32 slide projectors bring you the spirit and history of San Francisco, from the gold mines to the building of the Golden Gate Bridge and on to the present. Experience the San Francisco earthquake and fire of 1906 and a Chinese New Year's parade. The San Francisco memorabilia, nickelodeons, and games make waiting in the lobby for the next show a pleasure.

Pier 39 is a shopping/restaurant complex set right on the water. There's a double-decker merry-go-round and games arcade for the children. Sailing sessions and lessons and buggy and rickshaw rides are available. On weekends, street entertainers stroll the boards.

❧ Japan Center

With stores and restaurants, the Japan Center *(Nihonmachi)* can really be another world. The Peace Plaza with its reflecting pools and five-tiered Peace Pagoda is the center of entertaining festivals and celebrations during the year. You can see music and dance programs as well as judo, karate, and kendo matches. Inside the center, you can fish for an oyster with a pearl in it or have a Japanese fish-shaped *tai yaki*, a warm, filled, wafflelike pastry. Kids like the Sanrio "Hello Kitty" store.

Introduce them to sushi at **Isobune** (1737 Post Street, San Francisco 94115. 415 563-1030; W). Here you sit in front of a circular stream. Boats float by you carrying little plates of sushi. You take off what looks good, and pay by the plate. Start with the *ebi*, cooked shrimp, the *tamago*, or sweet omelet, or the California roll of crab and avocado. My nephew was hooked on the *unagi*, broiled eel with a barbecue sauce.

❧ San Francisco Fire Department Museum

655 Presidio Avenue (between Pine and Bush), San Francisco 94115. (415) 861-8000 ext. 365. Thurs.–Sun, 1–4, and by appt. Free. W.

Awe-inspiring photos of today's fire fighters mingle with uniforms, bells, trophies, and mementos of men and machines, the silver speaking trumpet, leather buckets, a buffalo-leather fire hose, and other relics of yesteryear. Lillie Coit, the darling of the San Francisco Fire Department, has her own case full of mementos. A 1912 fire chief's buggy, an 1890 American LaFrance Steam Fire Engine, and other machinery fill the room.

⇉ Fort Mason Center

Once a lonely barracks with deserted piers, Fort Mason, at the foot of Marina Boulevard and Laguna, is a flourishing center for the arts. Non-profit organizations from Greenpeace to Media Alliance are based here, and several performing arts groups give shows. **Greens**, a classy vegetarian restaurant, has a phenomenal view of the docks, the bay, and the Golden Gate Bridge (771-6222 for lunch and dinner reservations). The San Francisco Museum of Modern Art's rental wing is in Building A, as is the Dorothy Weiss Gallery and Fort Mason Art Center. The following (all San Francisco 94123) are of special interest to the young:

Museo Italo-Americano. Building C. (415) 673-2200. Wed.–Sun., 12–5 and by appt. Children under 12 are free, $2 for adults, and $1 for students and seniors. W. Preserves and displays Italian and Italo-American art, history, and culture in changing exhibits. Classes, community activities, and films are presented.

San Francisco African-American Historical & Cultural Society. Building C. (415) 441-0640. Wed.–Sun., 12–5. Adults, $1.75; children, 75 cents. School group rates. Tours by appt. Free. W. African-American artists and inventors are honored in the exhibit hall of this society. Clothing, African artifacts, pottery, historical documents, and crafts are displayed. Special rotating exhibits include one on black cowboys and another on Mammy Pleasant.

Mexican Museum. Building D. (415) 441-0404. Wed.–Sun., 12–5. Adults, $4; students, $2. Free first Wed. of the month, when it's open until 8. Tours by appt. Preconquest, colonial, folk, and fine art by Mexicans and Chicanos make up the changing exhibits in this well-designed museum. Family Sunday once a month offers free entertainment and workshops for children and their parents. School tours available.

Jeremiah O'Brien. Pier 3 E. (415) 441-3101. Weekends, 9–4. Adults, $2; seniors and children, $1; $5 per family. Parties. Volunteers welcome. Open Ship celebration weekends. Group tours. The last intact liberty ship carried food and ammunition to England, ferried troops during the Normandy invasion, and transported supplies to the South Pacific. Now it's back "home" where it was built, and has been restored to be shared with the public. On the third weekend of the month, the steam is up and the galley stove is working. Volunteers serve hot dogs, chocolate chip cookies, and lemonade, and kids can even blow the whistle.

❖ Haas-Lilienthal House

2007 Franklin Street (between Washington and Jackson), San Francisco 94109. (415) 441-3004. Guided tours Wed. at 12 and 3:15, and Sun. 11 through 4:15. Adults, $4; students and seniors, $2. Groups by appt. Walking tours.

This glorious Queen Anne Victorian, built in 1886, is a completely furnished memory of yesterday, right down to the cat on the sofa. Children of all ages will especially enjoy the train room.

❖ Octagon House

2645 Gough Street (at Union), San Francisco 94123. (415) 441-7512. Second and fourth Thurs. and second Sun. of each month, 12–3. Free.

Built in 1861, this unusual eight-sided home is the headquarters of the National Society of the Colonial Dames of America in California as well as a gracious museum of Colonial and Federal artifacts. A framed pack of Revolutionary War playing cards, a 13-star flag, dishes taken in battle by the USS *Constitution (Old Ironsides)* and a 1789 leather fire bucket from Philadelphia make this a pleasantly educational stop. Paper models of the house, 50 cents, are popular with young visitors. Next door is Allyne Park, a lovely picnic spot.

❖ Mission Dolores

3321 16th Street (at Dolores), San Francisco 94114. (415) 621-8203. Daily, 9–4 in winter, 9–4:30 in summer. Adults and group tours for those in the fourth grade or older, $1 suggested donation.

Built in 1776, the *Mission San Francisco de Asis*, as it is properly named, is the City's oldest structure. The unique Corinthian and Moorish architecture is not at all like other California missions. The cemetery contains the remains of some of the City's first settlers. To Alana, the "favorite part of the Mission was when you rang the bells in the Basilica."

❖ Josephine D. Randall Junior Museum

199 Museum Way, San Francisco 94114. Off Roosevelt, Upper Market Street area, at 14th Street, west of Castro. (415) 863-1399. Tues.–Sat., 10–5. Animal Room, 10:30–1 and 2–5. Free. Classes, workshops, nature walks.

High on a sunny hill overlooking the City, this museum and zoo is especially designed for children. Here they can watch a seismograph, see dinosaur bones and eggs, learn about the California Indians, and pat a live chicken. They can also talk to owls, hawks, and snakes, handle various minerals and ores, and learn about electricity. During one Saturday visit, youngsters were helping to clean the cages while a plump raccoon played on the front lawn. Members of the Golden Gate Model Railroad Club, located downstairs in the building, allow the public to watch them play with the model trains on the huge room-sized track, on the second and fourth Saturday of each month from 12 to 4.

❖ Golden Gate Park

From Fulton and Stanyan streets west to the ocean. The park office is in McLaren Lodge, San Francisco 94117. (415) 666-7200.

There are more than 1,000 acres of lakes and greenery in San Franciso's Golden Gate Park and at least l00 things to see and do. You can go boating or feed the ducks, cheer model boat races, picnic, ride horses, play tennis or golf or handball, go lawn bowling, watch the grazing bison, bicycle, skate, watch soccer and polo matches, pitch horseshoes, shoot arrows, play cards or chess, fly cast, or make water rings in the fountains. Stow Lake is the place to rent rowboats, motor boats, and pedal boats. Visit the magical, silvery Golden Gate pavilion from China, located on Stow Lake's island.

The Children's Playground, located on the Lincoln Avenue side of the park, features the slide with the fastest ride in the West, plus three other slides, geometrical shapes to climb (handicapped accessible), and swings.

The nearby **Herschel-Spillman 1912 Carousel** has been perfectly and wonderfully restored, with 62 menagerie animals, mostly in sets of two—cats, dogs, zebras, tigers, roosters, storks, giraffe, reindeer, frogs, pigs, goats, and beautiful horses—like Noah's Ark, plus a love-tub and a rocker (Wed.–Sun., 10–4:15; $1).

Older children might enjoy a walk through **Shakespeare's Garden** to identify the plants he wrote about. You can climb a drum bridge in the **Japanese Tea Garden** and then sit down to tea and cookies in the Tea House (Mon.–Sat., 9–6:30; adults, $2; children and seniors, $1; school tours: 415 666-7024).

Browse through the spun-sugar Victorian **Conservatory** on Kennedy Drive at any time of year to see displays of flowers in a tropical atmosphere (daily, 9–5; 415 386-3150; fee, parties). Ring the Mexican Bell in the **Strybing Arboretum's Garden of Fragrance**, where you can test your sense of smell, touch, and taste (weekdays, 8–4:30, weekends and holidays, 10–5; tours at 1:30, theme walks on Sat. at 1:30; 415 661-1316).

Gaze at the **Portals of the Past**, the marble columns that are all that was left of a Nob Hill mansion after the 1906 earthquake and are now the guardians of a duck-filled lake. Don't forget to say thank you to John McLaren—whose statue is tucked in a dell of rhododendrons across from the Conservatory, though he hated statues in parks—for turning sand dunes into an oasis of greenery gracing the City.

❧ M. H. de Young Memorial Museum

Golden Gate Park (north side of Music Concourse), San Francisco 94118. (415) 863-3330. Wed.–Sun., 10–5. Adults, $5; over 65, $3. First Sat. morning and first Wed. of the month, free. One charge admits you to the de Young, Asian Art, and Palace of the Legion of Honor museums on the same day. Lectures, events, docent tours, and school programs. W. The California Palace of the Legion of Honor is scheduled to reopen in early 1994.

The de Young's romantic Pool of Enchantment, with water lilies and a sculpted boy playing his pipes to two mountain lions, beckons visitors to this land of enchantment. There are paintings, sculpture, tapestries, and graphics by American, European, South American, African, and Oceanic artists. The Rembrandt is a favorite, and there is a lovely Mary Cassatt in the American section. The American Wing, donated by Mrs. John D. Rockefeller, houses the memorable *Rainy Season in the Tropics* by Frederick Church and several works by the Ash Can artists. A pleasant cafeteria with garden is open for lunch and afternoon tea.

❧ Asian Art Museum, Avery Brundage Collection

Golden Gate Park (north side of Music Concourse), San Francisco 94118. (415) 668-8921. Wed.–Sun., 10–5; until 8:45 P.M. Wed. Adults, $5; over 65, $3. Free, 10–Noon on Sat. and all day the first Wed. of each month. Tours by appt. W.

Chinese galleries on the first floor display objects from prehistoric times to the 19th century, including a magnificent collection of jade in a jewel-box setting, the Magnin jade room. Second-floor galleries exhibit art from Japan, Korea, India, Southeast Asia, Tibet, Nepal, and Iran. Both floors overlook the Japanese Tea Garden at the west end.

❧ California Academy of Sciences

Golden Gate Park (south side of Music Concourse), San Francisco 94118. Taped information, (415) 750-7145; switchboard, 750-7000. Daily, 10–5 winter and 10–7 summer. Adults, $6; ages 12–17, $3; ages 6–11, $1. Free the first Wed. of the month. Rates for groups by appt. Special programs and lectures. W.

Wander through the innovative Wild California Hall, the Hall of Gems and Minerals, and the Hall of North American Birds. Don't miss the Wattis Hall of Human Cultures; African Safari Hall with sights and sounds of Africa; and the Earth and Space Hall, with the Safe-Quake, a ride that simulates an earthquake. The Far Side of Science Gallery features the work of cartoonist Gary Larson.

Here you'll find **Morrison Planetarium**, a unique Sky Theater presenting a simulation of the heavens as seen from earth at any time—past, present, or future—on the 65-foot hemispherical dome. Special-effects projectors take the audience through space into whirling galaxies and black holes. Shows change regularly. For daily shows, call (415) 750-7141. There are shows on weekdays at 2; on weekends at 1, 2, 3, and 4. Adults, $2; ages 6 to 17 and seniors, $1; under 6 by special permission. "Exploring the Skies of the Season," $1 for all, is shown at noon on weekends and holidays. Closed Thanksgiving and Christmas.

Laserium is a "cosmic" laser show in which colorful images pulsate, float, and dance to music against a background of stars. Shows are on Thursday to Sunday evenings. Call (415) 750-7138 for titles, times, and prices. Not recommended for those under 6.

The whale fountain courtyard leads to the Academy's **Steinhart Aquarium**'s swamp, inhabited by crocodiles and alligators. Thousands of fish, reptiles, and dolphins live in 243 colorful tanks, all low enough for children to see into easily. Sea horses, black-footed penguins, deadly stonefish, piranhas, and shellfish of all colors, shapes, and sizes live here. Upstairs, the **Fish Roundabout** puts you in the middle of a huge tubular tank where fish swim quickly around you. Dolphins are fed every two hours; the penguins are fed at 11:30 and 4. For information, call (415) 750-7145.

❖ The Exploratorium

Palace of Fine Arts, 3601 Lyon Street, San Francisco 94123. Between Marina Boulevard and Lombard. (415) 561-0360. Tues.–Sun., 10–5; Wed., until 9:30. Closed Thanksgiving and Christmas. Also closed Mondays, except open on holiday Mondays. Adults, $7; seniors, $3.50; ages 6–17 and those with disabilities, $3. Members and those under 6, free. Tactile dome reservation: 561-0367. Groups: 561-0308. Parties. W.

This touchingthinkingpullingsplashingblinkingspinningopenclose-amazing museum of science, art, and human perception contains over 650 exhibits. It's the best combination of learning while playing in California. Clap and make a tree of lights blink, blow a two-foot bubble, learn about light, language, patterns, vision, color, and motion, and more. Laser beams, computers, holograms, stereophonic sound testers, and radio and TV sets are here to play with. Lively scientific exhibits demonstrate natural phenomena.

Cristy from El Portal Middle School wrote, "Thanks to you guys for even letting us touch things. Like an alien phone, a shadow screen, and a lot of lights!"

Across Marina Boulevard, at the end of the spit of land to the right of the St. Francis Yacht Club, is the **Wave Organ,** where you can sit and relax and listen to the activated voice of San Francisco Bay.

⇛ Presidio Army Museum

Presidio of San Francisco, Building 2, San Francisco 94129. (415) 561-4115. Tues.–Sun., 10–4. Groups by appt.: 921-8193.

Founded by Spain's military forces in 1776, the Presidio has flown Spanish, Mexican, and American flags. Cannon, uniforms, swords, and Army memorabilia tell the Presidio's 200-year history. Models and dioramas originally constructed for the 1939 World's Fair at Treasure Island depict the Presidio, the 1906 earthquake and fire, and the 1915 Panama-Pacific Exposition. Outside are artillery pieces and two restored "earthquake cottages."

⇛ Fort Point National Historic Site

San Francisco 94129. Foot of Marine Drive, on Presidio grounds, under San Francisco end of the Golden Gate Bridge. (415) 556-1693. Daily except holidays, 10–5. Guided tours and demonstrations by appt. Free.

Nestled below the underpinnings of the Golden Gate Bridge, Fort Point, which was built during the Civil War, is the only brick coastal fort in the West, the guardian of San Francisco Bay. With the icy Pacific slamming into the retaining wall and the wind whistling around the point, this is one of the coldest spots in the City. Two exhibits housed in the fort feature the contributions of women in the military and the history and achievements of black soldiers in the Army. Roam throughout the officers' and enlisted men's quarters, and walk through the huge casements where once were mounted more than 100 huge cannon. Ask one of the park rangers dressed in Civil War uniform to demonstrate how to load and fire a cannon. You may end up earning a cannoneer certificate. Check the schedule for special slide shows and a film telling how the Golden Gate Bridge was constructed.

❧ The Cliff House

1090 Point Lobos Avenue, San Francisco 94121. Geary Avenue and the Great Highway.

"A drive to the 'Cliff' in the early morning… and a return to the city through the charming scenery of Golden Gate Park tends to place man about as near to Elysian bliss as he may hope for in this world," wrote B. E. Lloyd in 1876. A drive to and from the Cliff House can still place you in Elysian bliss. It's still the best place in town to see the seals basking on Seal Rocks. There are restaurants with great views.

A **Visitors Center** downstairs (415 556-8642) shows the Cliff House in its various incarnations throughout the years, along with rotating natural history displays. Here you can also find information about Farallon Islands tours, visiting the Whale Center (654-6621), and other adventures.

The crammed **Musée Mécanique** (415 386-1170; daily, 11–7; 10–8 in summer) houses over 100 coin-operated machines, old and new. Swiss music boxes, a mechanical carnival, a mechanical 1920s farm, old-time movies, and music machines sit alongside electronic games and modern cartoon-themed challengers.

❧ San Francisco Zoo

Sloat Boulevard at 45th Avenue, San Francisco 94132. (415) 753-7083/ 753-7061. Daily, 10–5. Adults, $6.50; seniors and youth, $3; ages 6–11, $1; under 6, free. Zoo Keys, for audiotour, $1.50. Additional charge for children's zoo, merry-go-round, and zoomobile. Parties. Adopt-an-Animal programs. Summer junior volunteer programs. Group tours. Strollers for rent. Gift store. Picnic areas. W.

Do you have an urge to pet a hissing cockroach? Ride a zebra train? Walk through a tropical rain forest? San Francisco's state-of-the art zoo is a natural setting for happy, healthy animals and youngsters who enjoy learning about them. There are cassowary birds, white pheasants, black swans, kangaroos and koalas, Moulon and Barbary sheep, animals in the barnyard to be petted, and big cats who are fed every day at 2 P.M. except Monday (they don't eat every day in the jungle, either).

The Primate Discovery Center is five stories of open atriums full of swinging monkeys and apes. On the ground, the interactive exhibits provide for hands-on learning about the animals in front of you. Musk Ox Meadow and the Tuxedo Junction penguin pool are extremely popular, as is the Insect Zoo, where you can even pet a tarantula. "Bone Carts" bring certain birds and animals to visitors for close-up learning. The 1921 Dentzel Carousel near the entrance is still as beautiful and dream-inspiring as ever.

❖ Public Relations Tours

Basic Brown Bear & Company Teddy Bear Factory. 444 DeHaro Street, San Francisco 94107. At Mariposa on Potrero Hill. (415) 626-0781. Tours at 11 and 2, Saturday and by reservation. You can see 30 kinds of teddy bear cut and stuffed right in front of you—and even stuff your own. Factory outlet.

Levi Strauss Jeans Manufacturing Tour. 250 Valencia, San Francisco 94103. At 14th Street in the Mission district. (415) 565-9153. By appointment, 45-minute tours to see blue jeans made, from fabric to fanny.

MARIN COUNTY

Marin County is a land of mountains and seashore north of Golden Gate Bridge. Most of the "places" to go with children in Marin are natural wonders. You can drive to the top of Mt. Tamalpais and walk the trails overlooking miles of ocean, land, and city. You can explore the silent redwood groves of Muir Woods, then travel on to Stinson Beach or one of the lesser-known beaches for picnicking by the seaside, collecting driftwood, or wading in the icy sea. You can also spend hours fishing in the Marin lakes or hiking the beautiful Point Reyes National Seashore. And when you feel the need for civilization, you can head for the bayside villages of Tiburon or Sausalito, which will enchant the children as much as they do you.

❖ Marine Mammal Center

Fort Cronkhite, Sausalito 94965. From San Francisco: cross the Golden Gate Bridge, take the first exit after Vista Point, and follow signs to park entrance and beach. On the Marin Headlands in the Golden Gate National Recreation Area, near the batteries and bunkers on Rodeo Beach. (415) 289-SEAL. Daily, 10–4. Tours and classes. Free. Gift store. W.

The Marine Mammal Center is where we finally learned the difference between sea lions and seals. Sea lions have outer ear flaps; seals have small holes for ears. Sea lions walk on all four flippers and seals move on their bellies, like inchworms. The purpose of this center—which always needs volunteers—is to rescue and then release marine mammals stranded on the coastline. Stranded pups are bottle-fed herring milkshakes. (Please remember that just because a seal appears on the beach it doesn't necessarily need rescuing. Don't touch it unless you have a permit.) There are critters in cage-tanks to see, and informative illustrated panels to learn from. An exhibit center is in the works. After a recent visit, one third-grader sent this poem as a thank you:

> Dolphins are pink
> whales are red
> and seals blue and green like the ocean where they live.

The Bonita Point Lighthouse can also be reached through Fort Cronkhite. Although the light itself is way out on the rocks and worked by computer, you can reserve a tour, on weekends, at sunset, or during the full-moon walk, at (415) 331-1540. Free.

❧ Sausalito

After stopping for a moment to look back at the Golden Gate Bridge from Vista Point, spend a few hours in the Riviera by the Bay. Noted for years as an artists' colony, the village of Sausalito is now a mecca for tourists and young people. There are clothing and toy stores, ice cream parlors and coffee houses, art galleries and restaurants for every age, taste, and budget. The **Sausalito Historical Museum**, in the old City Hall on Litho Street, offers police and railroad memorabilia, period costumes, and vintage photos of the town (Wed. and Sat., 1–5, and Sun., 10–5; 415 332-1005; donation).

❧ San Francisco Bay–Delta Model

2100 Bridgeway, Sausalito 94969-1764. (415) 332-3870. Tues.–Sat., 9–4; summer weekends and holidays, 10–6. Free. W.

Cherol wrote, "Dear Ranger Suzette, Thank you for taking us on the tour. I learned about the tides. I just moved here from Utah, and this place is wonderful. Anyway, that movie was great. I hope I can come again. thank you." The U.S. Army Corps of Engineers has constructed a huge hydraulic scale model of San Francisco Bay and the Sacramento–San Joaquin Delta. The model shows the action of the tides, the flow and currents of the water, and the mixing of seawater and fresh water. Guided tours take 1 1/2 hours, but you can use the self-guided written information or the new tape-recorded audio program, which provides extensive information about the model and its operation. The model only operates when testing is scheduled, but there's so much to see—pictures, slides, models, and more—you'll be impressed.

The San Francisco Maritime National Historic Park runs the Bay Model and the "park" outside, where kids can visit *Hercules* the tugboat and the logging schooner *Alma*.

➤ Bay Area Discovery Museum

557 East Fort Baker, Sausalito 94965. From San Francisco: take Highway 101 north to Alexander Avenue exit, and follow signs. (415) 332-9646. In summer, Tues.–Sun., 10–5; in winter, Wed.–Sun., 10–5. Adults, $5; children, $3; seniors, $4. Parties. Discovery Cafe. Gift shop. W.

"The Bay Area Discovery Museum: A boppin' jammin' dancin' happenin' place to be!" So wrote Jez. And Fran called it a "Cool Place! Best museum in the world!" This hands-on museum for children and families is located in a spectacular setting at the foot of the Golden Gate Bridge. Its historic buildings house the permanent San Francisco Bay and Building the City exhibitions and art studio. The museum features ever-changing activities and workshops focusing on the arts and sciences. The surrounding area provides picnic spots, hiking trails, and tide pools for the entire family to enjoy. A not-to-be-missed attraction is the hand-made carousel created especially for the museum by master carousel maker Bill Dentzel.

➤ The Unknown Museum

Call Mickey McGowan at (415) 383-2726 for present location, times, and prices.

Kids of any age with an offbeat sense of humor will be entranced by this unique "visual newscast," a collection with Mr. Potato Head as its mascot. A piece entitled "TV Dinner" consists of an aluminum three-sectioned tray filled with television tubes and transistors. Each room is a dazzling and eccentric vision. A shrine to fast food can be flanked by hundreds of colorful school lunch boxes hanging from floor to ceiling—with Hamburglar and Ronald McDonald hanging between them. Childhood fantasies are augmented with an audio tape that mixes the obscure and the arresting, such as *Star Trek*'s William Shatner reciting "Mr. Tambourine Man" with elevator music. A visit here is a memorable experience.

➤ Tiburon

Named **Punta de Tiburon**, or Shark Point, by Spanish settlers, Tiburon is a quiet, one-street bayside village, a nice place to spend a sunny afternoon. Having lunch, indoors or out, while enjoying the view of the City from one of the restaurants on the bay can be heaven. Nautical shops, a Swedish bakery, and the bookstore are all fun to browse through. Our favorite restaurant is right next to the ferry landing: **Guaymas** (5 Main Street; 415 435-6300), for the kind of grilled fish and fowl you'd have in a seaside Mexican village. Hardy walkers can head up the hill to the **Landmark Society Museum in Old St. Hilary's Church** (1600 Juanita Lane, Tiburon 94920; Apr.–Sept. Sun. and Wed., 1–4, and by appt.; 415 435-1122; donation) to see a changing art exhibit and specimens of the local plants that grow nowhere else in the world. The Landmark Society also operates the new **China Cabin Museum** on the cove in nearby Belvedere. The 20- by 40-foot cabin, from the S.S. *China Cabin*, a steam sidewheeler, looks exactly as it did when it left New York for San Francisco in June 1867, on its first voyage (Wed. and Sun., 1–4; 415 435-2879; free).

❖ Richardson Bay Audubon Center

376 Greenwood Beach Road, Tiburon 94920. (415) 388-2525. Wed.– Sun., 9–5. Lyford House, Oct.–May, Sun., 1–4; $2. Public Nature Programs on Sun. Call for schedule.

Richardson Bay Audubon Center and Sanctuary provides a habitat for wildlife and is an environmental education center, a "window on the bay." Youngsters can explore the sea life and observe birds on nature trails. Programs, films, and classes help make visitors aware of the wonders around them. Lyford house is a Victorian mansion with period furnishings and Marin County history displays.

❖ Angel Island State Park

P.O. Box 866, Tiburon 94920. For tour information call the Angel Island Association, (415) 435-3522. For ferry schedules from San Francisco, call (415) 546-2815. Ferry from Tiburon daily in summer; on weekends or by arrangement in winter. Call (415) 435-2131. Adults, $5; children, $3; bikes, $1. For Ranger Station: 435-1915. Classes, tours, and groups, including disabled: (415) 435-3522.

Angel Island was the Ellis Island of the Pacific for Asian immigrants. Today, it's a wonderful place to spend the day or stay overnight (call for reservations). Most visitors ride the ferries to Ayala Cove, where lawn, beach, and barbecue pits beckon. The Visitors Center has interpretive nature and history displays, with a free 35-minute video. On weekends, April to October, Camp Reynolds, Fort McDowell, and the Barracks Museum at the Immigration Station are staffed by docents who'll give tours and tell stories. Young Alexis wrote: "When you first set foot on Angel

Island you see the green of the trees and the yellow of the houses but what you really see is the gray of the people...even though the colors may be of joy—you can feel the sorrow."

❖ Muir Woods National Monument

Muir Woods Road (off Highway 1), Mill Valley 94941. (415) 388-2595. Daily, 8 to sunset. Reservations for groups. Special events: 388-2596. Free. W.

This lovely forest of giant coast redwoods, some more than 200 feet high, is a breathtaking place to start the day. Among these magnificent trees, you'll encounter many other species of plant life, as well as an occasional black-tailed deer and, in summer, young salmon swimming through Redwood Creek. Naturalist John Muir wrote, "This is the best tree lover's monument that could be found in all the forests of all the world." A snack bar, gift shop, and ranger's station are near the park entrance. There are several self-guided trails, including one with signs in braille. Junior-ranger packs are offered free to young naturalists.

❖ Marin County Historical Society Museum

Boyd Park, 1125 B Street, San Rafael 94901. Off Third Avenue. (415) 454-8538. At this writing the museum was closed for earthquake repairs, so call for times and prices.

Designed to "stir the imagination and bring back panoramas of the past," this overstuffed museum displays original Mexican land-grant documents and mementos of the Miwoks, Mexicans, and pioneers who settled Marin. Lillie Coit's shoes, an early San Quentin oil lamp, and the military collection are notable. A favorite with youngsters is the huge tallow kettle at the entrance. Once used for boiling elk tallow for candles and soap at the Rancho Olompali, the area's original farm, the kettle was also used as a stewpot for the military during the Bear Flag War.

Just down the block is the **Mission San Rafael Archangel** (1104 Fifth Avenue; 415 454-8141; 11–4 daily, from 10 on Sun.; free). Inside the small chapel, the six flags under which the mission has served still fly: Spain, Mexico, the California Republic, the United States of 1850, the Vatican, and the United States of America.

❖ California Center for Wildlife

76 Albert Park Lane (off B Street), San Rafael 94901. (415) 456-7283. Daily, 9–5. Donation. W.

This small wildlife rehabilitation and nature education center cares for and releases back into the wilderness over 4,000 birds and animals a year. Volunteers are needed! The gist of the touch and guess boxes and other interactive exhibits is to show how wild animals interact with themselves and with humans. A little zoo exhibits animals that can no longer fend for themselves.

❯❯ Audubon Canyon Ranch

4900 Highway 1, Stinson Beach, 94970. From Stinson Beach, north 3 miles. (415) 868-9244. Mid-March to mid-July, weekends and holidays, 10–4, and by appt. Bookstore. Picnic areas. Free (donations welcome). W.

This 1,000-acre wildlife sanctuary bordering on the Bolinas Lagoon is a peaceful spot to view birds "at home." From a hilltop, you can watch the nesting activities of the great blue heron and the great egret. The ranch's pond, stream, and canyon are a living demonstration of the region's ecology—the delicate balance between plant and animal life and their environment. The display hall/museum shows local fauna and flora and offers information on the San Andreas fault.

❯❯ Point Reyes National Seashore

National Park Service, Point Reyes, CA 94952. On Highway 1 near Olema. (415) 663-1092. The park is never closed, but no overnight parking is allowed unless you're camping. Free.

When Francis Drake landed here in 1579, his chaplain wrote of a "Faire & Good Baye, with a good wind to enter the same." Today's visitors will agree. The beauty of the cliffs, the surf (swimmable in some places), the tide pools, lowlands, and forest meadows make you wonder why he went back to England. You can follow nature trails, birdwatch, backpack, picnic, rent horses, and camp. We like Drake's Bay best, and before we set out, we call the ranger's office there (669-1250) to check the weather. The cafe at Drake's Bay is nicely protected and even serves fresh oysters.

Start your visit at the **Bear Valley Visitors Center** (open 8–5 on weekends, from 9 on weekdays). You can get maps with suggested itineraries and all the information you may need while the kids watch a movie or slide show or explore the beautifully designed "walk-through diorama" of the world of Point Reyes. Our favorite of the interactive exhibits is a large log attached to a handle. When you press down, the log lifts up to show all the creepy-crawlies living underneath. Classes and special programs are listed on the schedule.

From Bear Valley, you can walk to the Morgan Horse Ranch (9–4:30 daily; 415 663-1763), along the Earthquake Trail, or to **Kule Loklo**, the replica of a coastal Miwok village. A granary, sunshade, sweat house, and *Kotcas*, "the place where real people live," have been reconstructed with authentic materials by volunteers. On weekends there are demonstrations on skills like hunting, sewing, weaving, and preparing acorn mush (sunrise to sunset; interpretive programs on request; 415 663-1092).

The Ken Patrick Visitors Center at Drake's Beach has displays on marine paleontology, 15th- and 16th-century exploration, Native Americans, and the marine environment. A saltwater aquarium has critters collected from the bay (415 669-1250).

The Point Reyes Lighthouse is open, with tours (Thurs.–Mon., 10–4:30). You have to walk down 300 steps to get there, because the light was meant to shine *below* the fog line on Marin's rocky coast. Since whalewatching is increasingly popular, and the best place around is the lighthouse, the park supplies free weekend shuttlebus service, January to March, from Drake's Beach to the Point Reyes Lighthouse (415 669-1534).

Tomales Bay State Park (daily, 8–8 in summer, until 6 in winter; 415 669-1140; $5 per car) has beaches for swimming and picnic facilities. The tide pools, rocky pockets that retain seawater when the tide goes out, provide endless hours of fascination—as long as you watch very quietly as the tide pool's occupants move through their daily routines. Seaweeds, anemones, barnacles, jellyfish, sand dollars, tiny fish, and flowery algae can hide if they want to!

❖ Johnson's Drake's Bay Oysters

Sir Francis Drake Boulevard, on the way to Drake's Bay in Point Reyes National Seashore. (415) 669-1149. Daily, 8–4:30.

Follow the crushed-oyster-shell driveway to the "farm" to see how oysters are raised—and buy a small succulent sample to taste in the sea air. Did you know that it takes 18 months for an oyster to grow?

❖ Tomales Bay Oyster Company

P.O. Box 296, Point Reyes Station 94956. 115479 Highway 1, Marshall. (415) 663-1242. Daily, 9–5. Picnic area and barbecue.

Families are welcome and, if the tide is out, rubber boots and old clothes are suggested for the kids who want to catch crabs and "slosh" in the mud looking at intertidal life. The farm is bordered by state park land that is open for hiking and exploring. Founded in 1909, TBOC is the oldest aquaculture facility in the state. Its many "fields" of stakes are spread out in the bay, each stake holding about 100 oysters. Different holding tanks hold seed, juvenile, and harvest-size oysters. Bay mussels are also grown on the farm. Kids love the bags of "empties." And the staff loves answering questions.

⇻ Marin Museum of the American Indian

Miwok Park, 2200 Novato Boulevard (P.O. Box 864), Novato 94948.
(415) 897-4064. Tues.–Sat., 10–4; Sun., 12–4. Docent tour Sun. at
1:30. Free.

"Thank you so much for being our guide! I would love to come back!
…I loved your visitors exhibit. I have been using my crow call a lot and
wearing my arrowhead necklace a lot too. I learned a lot about the artifacts and boat materials, clothing, food, money, and their religious ceremonies. I loved the diorama. I also enjoyed grinding acorns and drilling
holes into the soap stone. I was fascinated about what they wore for religious ceremonies. It was so very interesting examining their money, blan-
kets, and games. Hope to see you soon!" This was from Kylie, fifth grade.

The permanent exhibit, "Coast Miwok Indians: The First People
of Marin," explores local history and the interaction of early inhabitants
with the natural environment of Marin County. A "Touch Table" invites
visitors to participate in a hands-on experience. Temporary exhibits focus
on other aspects of Indian cultures of the western United States. Classes,
lectures, and films are offered, so call for schedules. The California Native
Plant Garden and surrounding park are super for nature walks and picnics.

To walk in the world of the Miwok, drive north on Highway 101 a
mile past the Marin airport to San Antonio Road, and cross west off the
highway to the Olompali State Historic Park, the former site of an old
Miwok Indian village.

In downtown Novato, the **Novato History Museum** (815 DeLong
Avenue; 415 897-1164; Tues.–Sat., 10–4; free), in the home of the town's
first postmaster, focuses on the history of Hamilton Air Force Base.

THE EAST BAY
ALAMEDA AND CONTRA COSTA COUNTIES

The East Bay, ranging along the east shore of San Francisco Bay, is dotted
with public parks and streams and crowned by Mt. Diablo. The places of
interest in this area are some distance from each other, so plan ahead and
call for up-to-the-minute times and prices. Boaters, fishermen, picnickers,
hikers, and nature lovers of all ages will find special places to visit here.

⇻ Navy, Marine Corps, Coast Guard Museum

Building 1, Treasure Island (off the Bay Bridge), San Francisco 94130.
(415) 395-5067. Daily except Christmas, Thanksgiving, and New Year's,
1–3:30. Groups by appt. Free. W.

Drive past one of the great views of San Francisco to an art deco masterpiece built for the 1939 World's Fair, and enter a large, airy collection of naval memories. The activities of the Navy, Marine Corps, and Coast Guard in Pacific waters from before the Civil War to tomorrow's space ventures are well presented. The Farallon Islands Lighthouse lens, a 1919 diver's suit, ship models, World's Fair mementos, and Pearl Harbor day photos are on display, and towering over them is Lowell Nesbitt's vast mural of the past, present, and future of American armed services in the Pacific.

✥ TJ's Gingerbread House

741 Fifth Street, Oakland 94607. Take the Broadway exit from Highway 880. (510) 444-7373. Luncheon at 12 and 1:30. Dinner, Tues–Fri. at 6 and 8:30; Sat., 4, 6, and 8:30. Gazebo downstairs (W) available for parties.

Hansel and Gretel's wicked witch would be envious of this restaurant, which looks good enough to eat. In a tiny shop downstairs, you'll find gingerbread cookies, puppets, dolls, T-shirts, soaps, tea—even gingerbread bubble bath. Upstairs, in a fantasy land of dolls—"a dream come true!"—TJ Robinson serves copious Cajun-Creole lunches and dinners to diners who order their main course when they make their reservations. Prices range from $16, for Bayou Spiced-Baked Catfish and "Spoon" Jambalaya, and up. We can vouch for the whiskey stuffed lobster, the rabbit piquante, the smoked prime rib, the cherry duck, and the Pick-Your-Heart-Out-Chicken. Each meal comes with fruit salad, Cajun comeback dirty rice, vegetables, sassy corn bread, beverage, and ice cream with a gingerbread cookie. For a nominal price, children can order just their own fruit salad, rice, and dessert.

✥ Ebony Museum

#30 Jack London Village, Suite 208-9, Oakland, 94607. (510) 763-0141. Tues.–Sun., 11–6. Donation. Gift shop. Tours by appt. W.

This grass-roots museum specializes in "soul" jewelry—necklaces of gold chitlins, fatback earrings, peanut pendants—as well as African and African American arts and artifacts. Benin royal tribal busts, 300-year-old Lobi ancestor figures from Zaire, and chieftain headdresses mingle with graceful wooden statues and rows of weathered masks. The "Degradation" collection of early racist art is an eye-opener, but the owner, Aissataui Vernita, believes in waking kids (and adults) up.

❯ Northern California Center of Afro American History & Life

Golden Gate Library, 5606 San Pablo Avenue, Oakland 94612. (510) 658-3158. Tues.–Fri., 12:30–5:30 and by appt. Free.

California's black Americans and their history are the theme of this lovingly put together collection that focuses on local families and recalls especially black American athletes, musicians, scientists, politicians, gold miners, cowboys, farmers, and doctors. Some of the people youngsters will "meet" here are Pio Pico, an early governor of California; black mountaineer James Beckworth; "Mammy" Pleasant; William A. Leidesdorff, who built one of San Francisco's first hotels and launched the first steamer in San Francisco Bay; and Colonel Allensworth, a black Army chaplain who founded one of the state's first black communities.

❯ The Oakland Museum

1000 Oak Street, Oakland 94607-4892. (510) 238-3401. Informational message: (510) 834-2413. Wed.–Sat., 10–5; Sun. 12–7. Closed holidays. Cafe. Gift shop. Free. W.

The Oakland Museum is three first-rate museums in one: California art, California natural sciences, and California history. You can always be sure of finding an afternoon's worth of interesting things for children of all ages.

One level concentrates on art from the days of the Spanish explorers to the present. Panoramic views of San Francisco and Yosemite, cityscapes and landscapes, and contemporary jewelry, ceramics, photos, paintings, and sculpture create a historic continuity in the visual arts.

The natural sciences gallery takes you across the nine zones of California, from the coast to the snow-capped eastern Sierra with its ancient bristlecone pines. Dioramas and displays of mammals, birds, rodents, and snakes in their native habitats provide fascinating replicas of the real thing. Three "information TV centers" in Cowell Hall provide instant answers to kids' questions with demonstrations and discussions by noted authorities.

Kids will like the California history level best of all. Begin with the Native Californians, the many Indian tribes, and walk through the superbly furnished "rooms" of the state's history, from the Spanish explorers and *Californios* to the gold miners and cowboys, the pioneers, the Victorian San Franciscans, and on to the California dream, from *Beach Party* to *American Graffiti* and the Summer of Love.

We always head for the 1890s shiny red fire pumper and the pioneer kitchen with the chair outside the glass—to bring the visitor into the picture. Concerts, films, and special exhibits are scheduled regularly. One young visitor wrote in the guest log, "I think that using junk to create art is very ingenious."

❧ Paramount Theater

2025 Broadway, Oakland 94618. Take Highway 980 to the Downtown exit. (510) 893-2300. Tours by appt., first and third Sat. of the month, 10 A.M. $1. Not advised for those under 10.

The Paramount, which has programs of interest to children, is the best example of art deco architecture on the West Coast. A metal grillwork ceiling teeming with sculpted life, gold walls with sculpted motifs from the Bible and mythology, and elegant embellishments almost compete with what's on stage.

❧ The Camron-Stanford House

1418 Lakeside Drive, Oakland 94612. (510) 836-1976. Tours Wed., 11–4; Sun., 1–5; and by appt. Donation. Children 12 and under free.

This 1876 Italianate-style Victorian, once the Oakland Museum, provides a look at Oakland history since the days of horse cars and gas lighting. Museum displays in the basement show local history as well as the restoration of the mansion. An interesting movie portrays the life of Franklina Gray Bartlett, who grew up and grew old in this home. Upstairs the elegant rooms have been restored to gracious splendor and include a portrait of Franklina as a 14-month-old bacchante and the newspaper stories about her wedding. Multimedia shows, special exhibits, and engaging curators add to the young visitor's enjoyment.

❧ Lakeside Park

Off Grand Avenue at Lake Merritt, Oakland 94612-4598.

A narrow strip of grass around Lake Merritt creates a peaceful oasis in the center of a busy city. In the Kiwanis Kiddie Korner, children can slide down an octopus or swing on a seahorse. The **Rotary Nature Center** offers an educational exhibit of native reptiles, mammals, and birds as well as an observation beehive (510 238-3739; Tues.–Sun., 10–5; Mon., 12–5; free).

Lake Merritt is the oldest wildlife refuge in the United States for free-flying waterbirds, which include an occasional pelican. Sailboats, houseboats, and paddleboats are available for renting. *The Merritt Queen*, a replica of a Mississippi riverboat, takes half-hour tours of the lake on weekends and in summer ($1 for adults, 50 cents for children and seniors). One young visitor wrote, "I enjoy your animals. The toad felt like mashed potatoes. I want to come back soon."

❯ Children's Fairyland

Lakeside Park, Lake Merritt, Oakland 94612. (510) 452-2259. Spring and fall, Wed.–Sun., 10–4:30; winter, Fri.–Sun. and school holidays, 10–4:30; summer, Mon.–Fri., 10–4:30, Sat. and Sun. until 5:30. Adults, $2.25; children, $1.75. Gift shop. Parties by reservation. Art classes and special events: (510) 832-3609.

Duck through The Old Woman's Shoe to meet Alice, the Cheshire Cat, and the Cowardly Lion. Then slide down a dragon's back or sail on a pea-green boat with the Owl and the Pussycat. Pinocchio, Willie the Whale, slides, mazes, rides, and enchanted bowers come to life. All the characters in Fairyland are here to make children smile, and a magic key unlocks their stories ($1). The Wonder-Go-Round, Magic Web Ferris Wheel, trains, and toyland bumper cars are nominally priced; puppet shows are free. Over 50 animals dwell here in storybook settings and many can be petted.

❯ Knowland Park–Oakland Zoo

9777 Golf Links Road, Oakland 94609. At 98th Avenue off Highway 580. (510) 632-9523. Park open 9–5 daily, except Christmas and Thanksgiving, weather permitting. Park admission: $2.50 per car. Zoo: 10–4 daily, later on summer weekends. Adults, $3.50; ages 2–14, $2; over 55, $1.50. Group discounts. Rides: 50 cents and $1. W.

This beautifully arranged zoo is one of the nicest in the state. Glide over the African Veldt and up into the hills on the 1,250-foot Skyfari Ride, or ride a miniature train for a breathtaking view of the bay. Over 330 animals from around the world make their home in 525 acres of rolling green parkland. The Children's Petting Zoo will make tots' barnyard tales come alive. Picnic, barbecue, and playground facilities are located throughout the park.

❯ Western Aerospace Museum

Oakland Airport North Field, P.O. Box 14264, Oakland 94614. At Doolittle Drive and Hegenberger. From Highway 880, west until you reach Doolittle, then right to Swan; left on Swan to Earhart, right on Earhart to Hanger 6, Alaska Airlines, then right onto Cook. (510) 638-7100. Weekends and holidays, 10–4. Adults, $3; students under 21, $2; under 12, free. Gift shop. W.

Ten antique and retired aircraft along with two Challenger forward command modules, a space shuttle, and a space shuttle simulation cabin can be seen in this exciting museum. There's also a Navy jet A-3 bomber, a Navy A-7 fighter, a torpedo TBM bomber, a Lockheed 10E like Amelia Earhart's (without the camera modifications), a Yugo trainer, an aerobatic flyer, and a Buker Jungmeister stunt plane. The pride of the fleet is the Short Solent, a large flying boat used in *Raiders of the Lost Ark*. Twelve exhibit rooms show flying photos and memorabilia.

❖ The Fortune Cookie Factory
261 12th Street (at Harrison), Oakland 94607. (510) 832-5552. Mon.– Sat., 10–3. Tours, 75 cents a person. Free cookies. Large groups by appt.

Fortune cookie machines are huge and black and make a lot of noise. You can see the flames inside them. Small round pans march relentlessly in and out of the flames. A giant dipper drops cookie batter into each pan, and by the time the rounds emerge, they are browned and just soft enough to bend. A lady grabs the soft round, puts a fortune in the cookie and folds it over a small metal bar, then sets it on a cooling rack. The fortune cookies even come in flavors. And you can write your own fortune.

❖ Dunsmuir House and Garden
2960 Peralta Oaks Court, Oakland 94605. Take the 106th Avenue exit from Highway 580. (510) 562-0328/3232. Apr.–Sept., first and third Sun. and every Wed., 11–4. Mansion tours Sun. at 12, 1, and 2; Wed. at 1. Grounds open Tues.–Fri., 10–4. Adults, $2; Seniors and youngsters, $1. Mansion tours including admission, adults, $3; seniors and youngsters, $2. Wednesday Tea in Dinkelspiel House by reservation. Tea and cookies on the veranda on Sun., as well as croquet and badminton. Special events, such as July Scottish Highland Games and the annual Christmas Show. Admission fees vary for special events: call (510) 562-3232.

This 37-room Colonial Revival mansion is set in a 40-acre estate in the East Oakland foothills. A visit will provide an enlightening sense of another way of life through architecture, photos, and garden strolls. Dunsmuir is the site of movies, weddings, and seasonal events.

❖ Chabot Observatory & Planetarium
4917 Mountain Boulevard, Oakland 94619. MacArthur Freeway and Warren Freeway. (510) 531-4560. Fri. and Sat., 7:30 P.M. Adults, $3; children, $2. Reservations advised (call 9–5, Mon.–Fri.). The Chabot Science Center is open irregularly, so call ahead.

The changing two-hour show here includes a movie, science demonstrations, planetarium program, and observation of the heavens through a large telescope. A recent show presented an exciting space voyage. Youngsters learn how astronomers explore the universe. Locating the Big and Little Dippers during the planetarium show is always a popular part of the program.

❧ Crab Cove Visitor's Center

1252 McKay Avenue, Alameda 94501. (510) 521-6867. Wed.–Sun., 10–4:30. Tours by reservation. Free.

This East Bay Regional Park District center is where the old Coast Guard Station was, on Crown Beach. The museum displays San Francisco Bay animals such as a saltwater hawk, a turtle snake, and a mountain toad.

❧ Alameda Historical Museum

2324 Alameda Avenue, Alameda 94501. (510) 521-1233. Call for programs, hours, and prices. Walking tours. W.

The official repository of objects relating to the history of the city, the museum owns collections of vintage clothing, household furnishings, toys, and art. The museum's pride and joy is quite modern, however. "Paint an Alameda House" is a hands-on exhibit of color design for older homes featuring computerized images of 16 of Alameda's homes. It's an electronic coloring book that teaches as it amuses.

❧ University Art Museum

2626 Bancroft Way, Berkeley 94702. (510) 642-1207. Wed.–Sun., 11–5. Ages 18–64, $5; ages 6–17 and over 65, $4. Free admission Thurs. between 11 and 12. W.

Berkeley's museum is a natural for children, not so much for the art but for the building itself. Its unique multileveled, concrete-slab construction enables a young visitor to see its spacious interiors from any of the many corners and balconies. The outdoor sculpture garden is fun and strikes a chord with young people. The Pacific Film Archive, located in the museum, shows classic, international, and children's films. Call (510) 642-1124 for schedules.

❧ Lawrence Hall of Science

Centennial Drive, University of California, Berkeley 94720. Up Hearst to the top of the university to Gayley Road, to Rim Way, to Centennial. Just south of Grizzly Peak Boulevard. (510) 642-5132. Mon.–Fri., 10–4:30; Sat. and Sun., 10–5. Adults, $4; students and seniors, $3; ages 3–6, $2. Galaxy Snack Bar. Parties. W.

There are young scientists who'd rather spend a day here than anywhere else in the world. The Lawrence Hall of Science has an outstanding variety of exhibits, science workshops, tests of your mathematical and logical ability, tests of knowledge, computers to play with, visual oddities, and a hundred different things to tantalize and amuse. Tots love the growling apatosaurus. Many kids are fascinated by the laser exhibit. Ocean Voyaging in Polynesia sweeps others away. The Biology Lab is the place to investigate the world of living things; the Wizard's Lab is for super experiments (both, weekends and holidays, 1:30–4:30; daily in summer). Holt Planetarium shows, the Science Discovery Theater, films, and special events offer ever-changing inducements to learning.

✦ Phoebe Hearst Museum of Anthropology

Kroeber Hall, Bancroft Way (at College Avenue), University of California, Berkeley 94720. (510) 643-7648. Tues.–Fri., 10–4:30; weekends, 12–4:30. Adults, $1.50; seniors, 50 cents; children, 25 cents. Museum Store.

Ten-year-old Mary wrote, "This place is really cool and interesting. I especially liked the rock statue of Phoebe Hearst. It was beautiful. I liked looking at the pottery too. P.S. How did you get all this stuff here?" Gena wrote, "I liked the head phones, the cows, and the baby carrier from Borneo." Many of the museum's rotating exhibits are developed from its vast holdings of ethnographic, archaeological, and archival materials. On occasion, the museum hosts nationally traveling exhibits of related interest to the fields of anthropology and ethnic studies. A visit will help children understand other peoples' worlds, past and present.

School groups may request tours of all major exhibitions and children's activity sheets will be provided. A special presentation on Ishi, the last Yahi Indian, is given for school groups year-round. In addition, a limited number of teaching kits that complement state-mandated social science curricula are available for loan at no charge. Reserve early! Lectures, movies, and slide presentations are also available.

✦ The Campanile

Sather Tower, University of California, Berkeley 94720. (510) 642-5215. Mon.–Sat., 10–3:30; Sun., 10–1:45. Fifty cents.

From the top of this tower, you can see San Francisco, Alcatraz, Mt. Tamalpais, the Golden Gate and Bay bridges, and the entire campus. Above you, 61 bronze bells, the largest weighing 10,000 pounds, ring out melodies three times a day. You can see them being played.

✦ Hall of Health

2230 Shattuck Avenue (lower level), Berkeley 94704. (510) 549-1564. Tues.–Sat., 10–4. Groups by appt. Drop-in visits encouraged. Free. W.

"Your body is yours for life...take care of it yourself" is the motto here. The Hall of Health, sponsored by Alta Bates and Children's Hospital in Oakland, is a free hands-on health museum full of interactive exhibits that encourage you to learn with all your senses. Kids can ride an exercycle that counts calories, manipulate a full-sized skeleton, put together a puzzle, listen to your heart beat, see how babies grow and are born, test your health knowledge on a computer, watch a movie, and much more. The Hall of Health sponsors a free child safety fair called KidSafe each year consisting of classes and ongoing exhibits such as Fire Safety, CPR, Personal Safety, AIDS Information, and Bicycle Safety.

❖ Tilden Regional Park

Canon Drive (off Grizzly Peak Boulevard), Berkeley 94708. (510) 525-2233. Nominal prices for rides, with varying times depending on the season. The Little Farm is open daily, 8:30–5. Free.

Tilden Park has a pony ride, historic merry-go-round, and miniature train. Native California botanical gardens, an Environmental Educational Center, wooded hiking trails, and swimming in Lake Anza are also popular. But the chief attraction for youngsters is the Little Farm in the Nature Area. Here they can meet barnyard animals like sheep, goats, cows, pigs, chickens, geese, rabbits, and a sociable donkey.

❖ Pixieland Park

2740 East Olivera Road (at Willow Pass Park), Concord 94519. (510) 689-8841. Daily in summer, and weekends in winter, 11–6. Rides 60 cents each, 10 for $5. Weekday ride bracelets.

This small amusement park is strictly for children ages one to eight. There are six rides—a merry-go-round, a train, a boat ride, a car ride, an airplane, Tubs of Fun, and a little Ferris wheel. There's a little concession stand and a picnic area reserved for birthday parties.

❖ McConaghy Estate

18701 Hesperian Boulevard, Hayward 94541. Off Highway 880 between Bockman and A streets. (510) 276-3010. Thurs.–Sun. 1–4 and by appt. Last tour at 3:15. (510) 278-0198. Adults, $2; seniors, $1.50; ages 6–12, 50 cents. Classes, $10. Special Christmas Program. Closed January.

This elegant 1886 farmhouse is so completely furnished it looks as if the family still lives here. One bedroom is filled with toys, games, books, and clothes used by a turn-of-the-century child. The kitchen displays an icebox, wood stove, and water pump. The dining room is lavishly decorated for each holiday. A tank house and a buggy-filled carriage house adjoin the house, handily located next to Kennedy Park with its picnic tables, merry-go-round, and train.

⋙ Hayward Area Historical Society Museum
22701 Main Street (at C), Hayward 94541. (510) 581-0223. Mon.– Fri., 11–4; Sat. 12–4. Closed holidays. Adults, $1; children, 50 cents. W.

The large brick 1927 post office is now a lovingly presented album of Hayward area history. Cameras, dolls, scrapbooks full of high school pictures, tax records and family albums, a 1923 fire engine, an 1820s hand-drawn fire pumper that was shipped around the Horn to San Francisco in 1849, a turn-of-the-century washing machine, a pump organ, and a 1930s post office present an engaging glimpse of the lifestyle of the past. The old phonograph can be wound up and played for youngsters, and the old stereopticon may be looked into. Exhibits change three times a year to keep visitors returning. A favorite is the holiday collection of toys, trains, dolls, Christmas ornaments, and cards.

⋙ Sulphur Creek Nature Center
1801 D Street, Hayward 94541. (510) 881-6747. Tues.–Sun, 10–5. Animal-lending library, 10–3. Donation. Picnic tables. W.

Sulphur Creek Park is a charming spot in which to introduce children to wildlife native to Northern California. Coyotes, raccoons, opossums, foxes, rabbits, skunks, hawks, owls, song and garden birds, a variety of reptiles and amphibians, and invertebrates are displayed in natural habitats. There are changing exhibits and a wildlife garden. Nature study classes, wildlife rehabilitation, and volunteer opportunities are available.

⋙ Hayward Shoreline Interpretive Center
4901 Breakwater Avenue, Hayward 94545. (510) 881-6751. Daily, 10–5. Free. Summer day camps.

Located on the Hayward shore of San Francisco Bay, this center is the hub of an 1,800-acre marshland park. You can explore marine life in a hands-on Wet Lab, search for animal life under the microscope, see a variety of exhibits on the shoreline area, check out a free family discovery pack or binoculars, and hike on eight miles of trails. Public naturalist programs on weekends.

⋙ Ardenwood Farm
Ardenwood Regional Park, 34600 Ardenwood Boulevard (at Highway 84), Fremont 94555. (510) 796-0663/796-0199. Apr.–Nov., Thurs.–Sun., 10–4. Adults, $5; ages 4–17, $2.50; seniors and disabled, $3. House tours

by appt. and on a first come–first served basis. Hay rides and wagon rides. Closed holidays. Rain may close the park. W (limited).

We've gotten more letters about Ardenwood Farm than any other place in this book, and it leaped onto our "top 11" list on the first visit. The 205-acre farm is a look into the Bay Area's farming past. Its motto:

May learning, science, useful art,

Adorn thy life, improve thy heart.

May kind affection, love so dear,

Hereafter bless, and guide you here.

At Ardenwood kids can visit a remarkably well restored Victorian farmhouse, built in 1857 by George Patterson, a '49er who found gold in the land. Costumed docents tend the Victorian flower garden, demonstrate such crafts of the Victorian era as lacemaking, and show off farming skills such as barrel making. Farm produce and flowers can be purchased. Buggy and wagon tours are popular, as are the horsecars, stages, and the Deer Park train. There are lots of animals in the farmyard and there's an Ohlone Indian village and burial site to see. There are picnic and party areas, and concerts are given in the gazebo.

❧ Mission San Jose

43300 Mission Boulevard, Fremont 94539. (510) 657-1797. Daily, 10–5. Closed holidays. Donation. Group tours by reservation. W.

"Dear Mission San Jose, I appreciated you letting us come to your mission. It was fun and exciting to see how the missioners lived and I liked the slide show about the mission and the church. I had a good time. My favorite thing was the fountain and the olive trees. Thank you very much. Sincerely, Lakisha."

Founded in 1797, Mission San Jose holds an exciting place in California history. A highlight of the museum tour is an exhibit on the Ohlone, the native people of the Bay Area. Father Duran, who arrived in 1806, taught some of the 2,000 Ohlone neophytes to play the original mission bells and musical instruments now on display. Original mission vestments, the original baptismal font, a pioneer cradle, and the sanctus bells are housed in the adobe living quarters of the mission padres. The mission church has been carefully reconstructed from hand-hewn beams and more than 180,000 adobe bricks.

❧ San Francisco Bay National Wildlife Refuge

Highway 84, Fremont 94539. At the east end of the Dumbarton Bridge, near the toll plaza off Thornton Avenue (510) 792-3178. Visitors Center, 10–5 daily. Free.

Weekend interpretive programs, nature study walks, slide and film presentations, and a self-guided trail through the marsh and diked ponds help introduce youngsters to the world around them. Discover packs are available free for check out and further exploratory fun.

Stephanie rhapsodized: "Thank you for the presentation you gave us. I like making tule rope. Angie and I made 4 ropes. When I looked through the binoculars I saw a squirrel and a white rabbit. I also saw ducks on the pond. When we played predator or prey I guessed them quickly. When I was on the bus I saw a snowy egret. I went on the board-walk with Michelle's grandfather. We saw pickle weed and we smelled sage. It smelled good. I liked the Indian games with stick, dice, marble game, and the relay game too. The stuffed animals looked like they were alive. I liked the way the pheasant felt. I liked the noisy musical instrument. It sounded like an airplane propeller....It was interesting to see and learn how the Indians cooked, fished, caught things, and played games. Right then I knew it was difficult to live in the Indian times. I hope I can come again sometime."

❖ Wind Farms of Altamont Pass

On windy days you can often hear them before you see them —the more than 7,500 giant wind turbines, perched on towers, on either side of Interstate 580. The world's largest "wind farm" produces electricity from the wind. A seven-mile drive just north of and paralleling I-580, begun either from Greenville or Mountain House roads, east of Livermore, tours the heart of the wind farms.

❖ Livermore History Center
2155 Third Street, Livermore 94550. (510) 449-9927. Wed.–Sun., 11:30–4. Free.

This exhibit on the history of the Livermore Valley from prehistoric times to the present is housed in the old Carnegie Library. Pictures, maps, artifacts, and mementos from local families, businesses, and groups are on display. A 19th-century drugstore exhibit has been installed. The museum members are currently working on the restoration of the historical Duarte Garage/Lincoln Highway Museum in Livermore at North L Street and Portola. Early-day fire trucks, wagons, and other apparatus can be viewed by appointment.

Ravenswood, the Victorian-era home and gardens of San Francisco's "Blind Boss" Christopher Buckley, is occasionally open to the public (on Arroyo Road; call (510) 373-5770 for an appointment). Visitors will see cloisonne chandeliers, an ornate billiard table, clothing, pictures, and mementos of the Buckley family.

❯❯ Lawrence Livermore National Laboratory

7000 East Avenue (P.O. Box 808), Livermore 94550. Visitors Center: Around the corner from the main entrance, on Greenville Road, between East Avenue and Highway 580. (510) 422-9797. Mon.–Fri, 9–4; Sat., 12–5. Closed holidays. Computer Museum: 1401 Almond Avenue, off East Avenue a block from LLNL. (510) 423-7015. By appt., 10–5. Picnic areas. Free. W.

"How does a computer talk?" "What's a 'Star Wars' weapon?" "Can scientists make something as hot as the sun?" The answers to these and many other intriguing questions about science can be found at Lawrence Livermore National Laboratory's Visitors Center. Hands-on exhibits, displays, films, audio tapes, and a multimedia show explain the laboratory's mission. Visitors will learn about lasers, fusion energy, biomedical and environmental research, energy, and resources.

The laboratory has just opened a **Computer Museum**, which displays photographs, computer parts, and hardware and software that can actually be used. Computers are explored from the ancient past (1953) to the present.

❯❯ Amador-Livermore Valley Museum

603 Main Street, Pleasanton 94566. (510) 462-2766. Wed.–Fri., 11–4; Sat. and Sun., 1–4. Free. W.

Housed in the 1914 Town Hall, this museum features platform exhibits of yesteryear including a blacksmith shop. Changing cultural exhibits explore the Tri-Valley area's history from fossil remains to the present. The Museum Art Gallery exhibits change regularly and feature local artists in all media.

❯❯ The Museums at Blackhawk

3700 Blackhawk Plaza Circle, Danville 94506. (510) 736-2280. Information: (510) 735-2277. Tues.–Sun, 10–5; Wed. and Fri., until 9. Behring Classic Car Museum: adults, $5; students and seniors, $3; 6 and under, free. The UC Berkeley Museum: adults, $3; students and seniors, $2. Combined admission, $1 off the Car Museum price. Lectures, programs. Tours by appt. W.

The Behring Classic Car Museum shows rare classic automobiles as works of art. It showcases Kenneth Behring's $100-million collection of custom-built and one-of-a-kind automobiles created during the years between the two world wars. There are rotating exhibits and video inter-active presentations with the designers of the Tucker, Duesenberg, 1955 Ford Thunderbird, and other classics.

The UC Berkeley Museum is a showcase for artistic vision, for living history and prehistory, and for scientific discovery. "The Artistic Spirit" offers selections from the Lowie collection of artifacts dating back to 3500 B.C. There are Nigerian wooden figures, Peruvian ceramics, Egyptian coffins, and hundreds of treasures to explore, along with quizzes, fossil digging sections, and other hands-on exhibits. The museum is especially proud of a nine-million-year-old mastodon found just two miles away in the Blackhawk Quarry Site.

❧ Richmond Museum
400 Nevin Avenue (P.O. Box 1265), Richmond 94802. (510) 235-7387. Thurs., Sat., and Sun., 1–4, except holiday weekends, and by appt. Free. W.

Life in the Richmond area up to the mid 1940s is portrayed in the history gallery with the aid of room re-creations, photographs, panel dis-plays, and text. Old-time vehicles such as a peddler's wagon and a Model A Ford are a thrill to young and old alike. In addition to the permanent history gallery, changing exhibits draw on a wide variety of topics of local interest.

❧ Diablo Valley College Museum & Planetarium
321 Golf Club Road, Pleasant Hill 94523. Off Willow Pass Road from Highway 680. (510) 684-1230 ext. 330. Hours change each semester. Groups by appt.

In this museum youngsters can see a seismograph working, a Fou-cault pendulum swinging, and changing oceanography and anthropologi-cal exhibits on Native Americans. Local animals, especially the nocturnal moles, weasels, and owls, are fun to see, as are the star shows.

❧ The Lindsay Museum
1901 First Avenue, Larkey Park, Walnut Creek 94596. Highway 680 to Geary, left onto Geary, left onto Buena Vista, right onto First Avenue. (510) 935-1978. Wed.–Sun., 1–5. Free. W. Wildlife Rehabilitation training for ages 16 to adult.

One young fan, Bobby, wrote, "I liked the turtle and the king snake, but what I liked one of the most was the guinea pig." Exploring the rela-tionship between people and wildlife is the theme of the Lindsay, soon to be in a new building. Local animals are brought to the museum and nursed to health; if they can be released, they are, but many end up as permanent residents.

To underscore the living conditions of urban wildlife, the museum displays them in a city context. The aim is to help people understand how animals do and don't survive when development encroaches on their natural habitat. Some of the animals can be petted. The museum's discovery room, crowded with opportunities for hands-on learning, features a real oak tree, discovery boxes, and a demonstration stage. The Pet Library allows museum members to borrow a rabbit, rat, or guinea pig for a week. The museum also offers tours, school visits, classes, and trips. Volunteers of all ages are always needed in the Wildlife Department, which cares for 7,500 hurt animals a year.

History buffs will also want to visit **Shadelands Ranch Historical Museum**, a few blocks away, a restored time capsule/home with a gazebo in back at 2660 Ygnacio Valley Road, Walnut Creek 94598 (510) 935-7871; Wed., 11:30–4; Sun., 1–4; adults, $2; picnics and parties; W.

❧ Eugene O'Neill National Historic Site

P.O. Box 280, Danville 94526. Tours by reservation only, at 10 A.M. and 12:30 P.M. (510) 838-0249.

Tao House, built in 1937, is where Eugene O'Neill wrote *Long Day's Journey into Night* and *A Moon for the Misbegotten*. It's now a museum run by the National Park Service and will interest high school and college students. The dark blue ceiling, white concrete walls, and deep red floors give the place an Oriental air with art deco accents. O'Neill's study, with two desks, ship models, sharpened pencils, and a wastebasket full of crumpled paper, captures the author's life. The beauty of the Las Trampas Hills surrounding echo the solace O'Neill found here.

❧ The Alvarado Adobe & Blume House Museum

1 Alvarado Square, San Pablo 94806. At the intersection of San Pablo Avenue and Church Lane. (510) 215-3080. By appt. Donation.

The Alvarado Adobe has been precisely reconstructed on its original site. The owner, Juan Bautista Alvarado, husband of Martina Castro, was the Mexican governor of California in 1840 and lived here until 1882. The house itself was built in the early 1840s by the Castro family. Furnished in a mix of Rancho and Early California styles, it offers visitors showcases of artifacts including *cascarone*—painted eggshells that were filled with confetti or cologne and cracked open on fellow party-goers. And from local Indian mounds there are Indian shell games and samples of *amole*, the soap plant, which was roasted and eaten; boiled for glue; pounded into a paste that stupefied fish when thrown into a stream; used for twine, shampoo, and soap; and dried to stuff mattresses.

The Blume Museum is a 1907 farmhouse now refurnished to look as it did then, with oak furniture, early plumbing fixtures, and an iron stove in the kitchen.

⧸ Crockett Historical Museum

900 Loring Avenue, Crockett 94525. On the water's edge in the old railroad depot. (510) 787-2178. Wed. and Sat., 10–3. Free.

Pictures, medals, trophies, a stocked kitchen, model ships, and memorabilia of oil fields of the 30s are just part of this admirable collection.

⧸ Benicia Capitol State Historic Park

First and G streets (P.O. Box 5), Benicia 94510. (707) 745-3385. Daily, 10–5. Closed Tues. in winter and closed holidays. Adults, $2; ages 6–18, $1.

Benicia was the first capital of California, and it still looks much like it did in 1853. The exhibit rooms capture a bit of California history— right down to the whale-oil lamps, quill pens, shiny brass cuspidors, and varied headgear on all the desks. The Senate is on the first floor, the Assembly on the second. Interactive displays also bring the past to life.

The **Fischer-Hanlon House** next door is also part of the state historic park complex. This fine old federal-style house has been lovingly restored by volunteers, including the creamery and the carriage house with buggy and cart (with horses and manure). This is a proper, upper-class merchant's home of the 1880s, and the Hanlon sisters enjoyed it until they gave it to the state (weekends, 12–3:30).

Don't forget to go across town to the **Camel Barns**, in the Arsenal on Camel Road off Park. These large sandstone warehouses now serve as nicely designed art galleries and a historical town museum, but they actually housed 35 Army camels from 1856 to 1864. A donation is requested, and tours are by appointment only (open weekends, 1–4; also Fri. in summer; 707 745-2841; W.)

⧸ John Muir National Historic Site

4202 Alhambra Avenue, Martinez 94553. Off John Muir Parkway. (510) 228-8860. The house is open for self-guided tours Wed.–Sun., 10–4:30. Guided tours and Environmental Living Programs by reservation. $1.

"I hold dearly cherished memories about it [the house] and fine garden grounds full of trees and bushes and flowers that my wife and father-in-law and I planted—fine things from every land. . . ."

The book John Muir wrote these words in is still in his office. After a beautiful film narrated from John Muir's text and scenes of the natural wonders that inspired it, visitors tour Muir's large 19th-century ranchhouse, one of the most authentically presented houses you can visit. The closets are still filled with clothing. Muir's suitcase is on the bed, ready for travel; his glasses and pencils are on the desk in his "scribble den." Pictures of his friends President Theodore Roosevelt and naturalist John Burroughs are on the walls, and you can look through some of the scrapbooks in the parlor. You can go up to the attic and ring the ranch bell in the bell tower.

The **Martinez Adobe**, built by the son of the Mexican don for whom the town was named, is in the garden, where you can wander at will. Muir's daughter and her family lived there. Muir also advised, "Climb the mountains and get their good tidings. Nature's peace will flow into you as sunshine flows into trees. The winds blow their open freshness into you, and the storms their energy, while cares will drop off like autumn leaves." This is a good place to start.

❖ Black Diamond Mines Regional Preserve

5175 Somersville Road, Antioch 94509. Take Highway 4 to Somersville Road and head south on it toward the hills. (510) 757-2620. One- and two-hour tours by reservation. Children under 7 not permitted underground. Ages 12–61, $3; 7–11 and over 62, $1.50. Miner's hardhats and lights provided; wear a jacket and sturdy shoes.

Black Diamond Mines Regional Preserve was the site of 19th-century coal mining and 20th-century sand mining. The Hazel-Atlas sand mine on the property has been preserved as an underground mining museum for your enjoyment. It's the only place in the area where you can go into a mine and through the tunnels.

The surrounding 4,100-acre preserve was once home to three thriving towns. Now, only Rose Hill cemetery, ruins, and trails remain. Historic photographs and videotapes on the area's history are available for viewing daily, 8 A.M. to dusk.

❖ Pittsburg Historical Society

40 Civic Avenue (Off Richmond), Pittsburg 94565. (510) 439-7501. Sun., 1–4:30 and by appt. Donation.

"Were it not for the preservation of memorabilia, the history of this area would fade and pass without record." This is the motto of the Pittsburg Historical Society.

Gifts from local families have helped make this collection a fine one.

THE PENINSULA AND SAN JOSE AREA

The Peninsula and the San Jose area provide many days of happy "attraction" hunting. From the huge amusement park, Great America, to small historical museums, such as Lathrop House in Redwood City, the area is full of surprises, including some new Silicon Valley–inspired exploration museums. Since the area grows ever more crowded and less suburban, city street maps are especially helpful.

✤ Sanchez Adobe

1000 Linda Mar Boulevard (off Highway 1), Pacifica 94044. (415) 359-1462. Tues. and Thurs., 10–4; Sat. and Sun., 1–5 and by appt. Free.

In 1842, the *alcalde*, or mayor, of San Francisco, Señor Sanchez, built his home in the farmland that once produced food for San Francisco's Mission Dolores. The adobe still stands, filled with artifacts from the Costanoan Indians who lived here first, Sanchez's rancho mementos, and the Victorian furniture and clothes of several Sanchez generations. Today's youngsters can participate in hands-on programs such as adobe brick making, Indian games, and Indian skills workshops put on by the San Mateo County Historical Association.

✤ Phipps Ranch

2700 Pescadero Road (P.O. Box 349), Pescadero 94060. (415) 879-0787. Daily, 10–6; until 7, Easter to Halloween. Free. Tours, by appt., $1.

This working farm, with a roadside stand, nursery, barnyard, gardens, and picnic areas, makes a very pleasant outing. Pick-your-own berry and vegetable sections can be a happy challenge. While parents buy fresh produce, herbs, an intriguing selection of dried beans, and plants in the nursery, kids can explore out back. There are several large aviaries filled with colorful, exotic birds. In the barnyard is Eyore the donkey, a black cow named Duchess of Midnight, several momma goats and their broods, and a poultry pond area filled with swans, ducks, and pheasants. There are ponies to ride and the star of the show is an enormous Chinese pig named Arnold.

✤ Coyote Point Museum for Environmental Education

1651 Coyote Point Drive, San Mateo 94401. Coyote Point Park, off Poplar Avenue from Highway 101. (415) 342-7755. Tues.–Sat., 10–5; Sun., 12–5. Closed Christmas, New Year's, Thanksgiving, and Thanksgiving Fri. Adults, $3; seniors, $2; ages 6–17, $1. First Wed. of the month, free. Gate fee for park, picnic areas, playgrounds, and beach: $4 per car. W.

The Environmental Hall is devoted to the understanding and appreciation of nature and our place in it—with a specal emphasis on the preservation and protection of the earth's resources and creatures. Computers and other hands-on games, models, and exhibits serve to educate visitors about the environment. The separate Wildlife Habitats house mammals, birds, amphibians, and reptiles native to the Bay Area in their natural setting. There are inside and outside viewing areas with a walk-through aviary.

✦ Japanese Tea Garden

Central Park, San Mateo 94403. (415) 377-4640. Mon.–Fri., 10–4; Sat. and Sun., 11–5. Free. W.

This proper, gracious Japanese garden is a soothing spot in the midst of city bustle. Quaint bridges and rock pathways take the visitor past a waterfall, a pond thick with waterlilies and *koi* (carp), and in the springtime, pink cherry blossoms. The teahouse is open, irregularly, in summer.

✦ San Mateo County Historical Museum

1700 West Hillsdale Boulevard, San Mateo 94402. Off Highway 101 at Route 92. (415) 574-6441. Mon.–Thurs., 9:30–4:30; Sun., 12:30–4:30. Free.

A walk through this museum is a walk through history. You begin with the Pleistocene period—14 million years ago—and view bones and fossils from that age found in San Mateo. Then on to the Costanoan Indians of 3,000 years ago, and the description of their magic dances, boats, tools, and food. The Mission Rancho period is well represented. Exhibits of lumber mills, an old general store and bar, settlers' wagons, and unicycles recall the past. Galleries change exhibits to focus on such subjects as 19th-century fire fighting, the many mansions of San Mateo, and transportation. There are also lectures and audiovisual programs.

✦ Lathrop House

627 Hamilton Street, Redwood City 94063. (415) 365-5564. Tues.–Fri., 11–3. Donation.

In 1863, Benjamin G. Lathrop, the county's first clerk, built this handsome Gothic Revival mansion, "Lora Mundi," on a lot bought from the Arguello family.

The house has been relocated twice and has been restored—right down to the top hats on the hall rack—by the Redwood City Heritage Association. The ground floor kitchen is equipped with a woodburning stove and butter churn.

❖ Marine Science Institute

*1200 Chesapeake Drive, Redwood City 94063. (415) 364-2760. Mon.–
Sat., 8–5. Call for prices of the shoreside and boating programs.*

"I enjoyed geo/chem—using the VanDorn bottle to get water samples
and sticking your fingers in 'Benthic Oooze'! I liked putting out the otter
net and catching the fish and giving birth to some fish. I thought that
looking at Phytoplankton, Zooplankton, and Circumplankton was fun."
This is one San Jose student's response to the four-hour Discovery Voyage
on the 85-foot research vessel *Inland Seas*. Groups of 40 to 45, over 10
years old, learn about marsh and marine life and the sea around us.

❖ Filoli House and Gardens

*Cañada Road, Woodside 94062. Filoli Nature Hikes: Individual and group
tours and nature hikes by reservation; (415) 364-2880/366-4640. Fee.
Children must be accompanied by an adult.*

Explore the many trails in the remote areas of Filoli. You can learn
about the Indians who lived here many years ago and touch the San
Andreas fault line. Learn about the animals, plants, ecosystems, and history of a fascinating place in the Bay Area. The two-hour hikes are two to
three miles long. Filoli's House and garden tour is not open to children
under the age of 12, including babies in backpacks and strollers. Gustavo
wrote, "I had a real good time....My favorite part was when we went to
the wild life center. I also liked the Indian dig. Even if we didn't really see
a turkey vulture or a red tailed hawk, the turret spider was pretty amazing!"

❖ The Woodside Store

*Kings Mountain and Tripp roads, Woodside 94062. (415) 851-7615.
Tues., Thurs., Sat., and Sun., 12–5. Tours by appt. Free.*

The San Mateo Historical Society has preserved, stocked, and
opened the 1850s lumber/general store that opened in 1853 as a stage
stop. A slide show explains more of the site history.

❖ NASA Ames Research Center

*Moffett Field 94035. Off Highway 101. (415) 604-6274. Visitors Center
open Mon.–Fri., 8–4:30; free. Outdoor two-hour tours, two miles long, by
appt., for those over age 9: (415) 604-6497. Closed federal holidays. Gift shop.*

After an orientation lecture and film, visitors can see the world's
largest wind tunnel, centrifuge operations, research aircraft, or flight
simulation facilities, depending on the center's schedule. In one section,
tiny robots roam in a simulated lunar landscape. The center focuses on
space exploration and artificial intelligence, developing new ways to link

humans and the highly advanced computers needed for the future space missions now on NASA's drawing boards. Films, telelectures, and school presentations are also available.

❧ West Bay Model Railroad Association

1090 Merrill Street, Menlo Park 94025. (415) 322-0685. Free.

Three different-sized trains run on the club's 2,000 feet of track, whistling past miniature towns and painted scenery and over tiny bridges and turntables. Adding to the effectiveness of the show is a tape of special sound effects interspersed with the story of how the club came about. The club also has a railroad-stationery display, a library, and a workshop. The members' special Christmas show on the second weekend in December is a favorite with local youngsters.

❧ Stanford University

Stanford University Campus, Stanford 94305. Highway 101 to Stanford exit. (415) 723-2300. Stanford Guide & Visitors Service, 723-2560/723-2053: Mon.–Sun., 10–4 when school is in session. Hoover Tower Observation Platform, 723-2053: Mon.–Sun., 10–4:30 when school is in session; adults, $1; children and seniors, 50 cents. Leland Stanford, Jr., Museum, 723-3469: call to be sure it's open. Stanford Linear Accelerator Center, 926-3300 ext. 2204: tours by appt., free. Jasper Ridge Biological Preserve, 327-2277: tours by appt., free. Campus walking tours, 723-2560: Mon.–Sun at 11 and 3:15, free.

In addition to the breathtaking view from the 250-foot-high observation platform at the top of the tower, the **Hoover Exhibit Rooms** display some of the treasures collected by Herbert Hoover and his wife, Lou Henry Hoover, and document some of their remarkable accomplishments. Among the items on display are a priceless gold Peruvian mask, one of Hoover's fishing rods, a model of the Hoover Dam, Lou Henry's Stanford diploma, and the original copy of one of the earliest Soviet American agreements (1921).

❧ Baylands Nature Interpretive Center

2775 Embarcadero Road (at the eastern end), Palo Alto 94303. (415) 329-2506. Tues.–Fri., 2–5; weekends, 1–5. Free. Groups by appt.

This bayside nature center is on pilings out in a salt marsh, handy for the nature walks and ecology workshops it excels in. The exhibits show local birds, plants, and a saltwater aquarium. On weekends, there are nature movies and slide shows, as well as nature and bird walks; bike tours; wildflower shows; fish, pond, and geology programs; and workshops.

❥ Palo Alto Junior Museum and Zoo

Rinconada Park, 1451 Middlefield Road, Palo Alto 94301. (415) 329-2111. Tues.–Sat., 10–5; Sun., 1–4. Free. W.

This beautifully constructed museum has constantly changing exhibits to keep kids coming back for more. Outside, in the poured concrete shelters, there are snakes and reptiles, ravens, owls, foxes, and lovable rabbits. Ducks nest under the bridge that curves over the pretty ponds. The exhibitions program focuses on physical, biological, and earth sciences.

❥ Barbie Doll Hall of Fame

Doll Studio, 460 Waverly Street, Palo Alto 94301. (415) 326-5841. Tues.–Sat., 1:30–4:30. Adults, $3; children, $1.

The world's largest collection of Barbie dolls—14,000 Barbies and Kens—includes the first black Barbie, a hippie Barbie, Barbie as the first woman astronaut, Barbie as yuppie, and other incarnations reflecting the changing fashions in clothes, accessories, and hairstyles over the last quarter century.

❥ Perham Electronics Museum Foundation

Sunnyvale. (408) 734-4453. Call for reservations.

Based on a private collection started in 1893 by six-year-old Douglas Perham, this is the most extensive display of early electrical and electronic devices in the West. Young scientists will be intrigued by exhibits of the first radio broadcast station, the first Silicon Valley electronics firm, the first TV picture tube (invented by Philo Farnsworth in San Francisco), a 10-foot robot, and hands-on demonstrations of electricity and magnetism.

❥ Sunnyvale Historical Museum

235 East California, Sunnyvale 94085. (408) 749-0220. Tues. and Thurs., 12–4:30; Sun., 1–4; and by appt. Free.

This sweet museum captures the past with artifacts and pictures of the pioneers.

❥ California History Center

De Anza College, 21250 Stevens Creek Boulevard, Cupertino 95014. (408) 864-8712. Mon.–Fri., 8–12 and 1–4:30; Sat., 10–2. Closed July and Aug. Free. Call for special Sat. hours. Group tours by appt.

Changing exhibits—from "First Californians" to "The Chinese in the Monterey Bay Area" to "Hard Rock Gold Mining"—explore California's rich and varied history. This living history museum is housed in the restored Le Petit Trianon, the original house on De Anza land. Visitors tour this elegant Louis XVI mansion, with a pavillion reminiscent of Versailles.

✦ Minolta Planetarium

De Anza College, 21250 Stevens Creek Boulevard at Stelling Road, Cupertino 95014. (408) 864-8814. Call for times and prices, since they change with each class session. Birthday parties. W.

The Minolta Planetarium uses the latest audiovisual and video projection systems to present remarkable family shows. The main projector spreads the night sky across a 50-foot dome, while sound penetrates the audience using a Bose full-spectrum system that includes two 16-foot-long sound cannons adding the dimension of feel to music and special sound effects. One hundred fifty other projectors produce dazzling effects, such as a flight to the moon with the astronauts or travel back in time to see the birth of a star. Family programs, which include preschool-age children, are a specialty.

✦ Hakone Japanese Gardens

21000 Big Basin Way, Saratoga 95070. (408) 867-3438 ext. 245. Mon.–Fri., 10–5; weekends, 11–5. Closed holidays. Donation. Children under 10 must bring an adult.

Walk along curving foliage-lined paths, pass through a wisteria-roofed arbor, and step on three stones to cross a stream next to three waterfalls. Climb a moon bridge to see the goldfish. Discover a moon-viewing house and gazebos hidden in the trees. Spy stone and wooden lanterns and statues of cranes and cats hidden in the flowers. This wonderful garden was designed by a former court gardener to the Emperor of Japan as a hill and water garden, the strolling pond style typical of Zen gardens in the 17th century. The teahouse is open by appointment.

✦ Villa Montalvo

Saratoga–Los Gatos Road, Saratoga. (408) 741-3421. Arboretum: Mon.–Fri., 8–5; weekends, 9–5. Galleries: Thurs.–Fri., 1–4; weekends, 11–4. Free.

Nature trails traverse a redwood grove, hills and meadows, and flower-covered arbors in this arboretum. The villa's grounds are also a bird sanctuary for over 60 species of birds. The villa takes its name from a 16th-century Spanish author. Montalvo wrote a novel describing a tribe of Amazons living in a fabulous island paradise named "California." The Amazons rode on gryphons, and the many stone gryphons on the grounds will entrance youngsters. Music, dance, and other performing arts events, many geared for children, such as storytelling, puppetry, and children's ballet performances, are scheduled throughout the year. The villa also hosts Environmental Volunteers classes in the spring and a performing arts camp each summer.

❖ Billy Jones Wildcat Railroad & Carousel

Oak Meadow Park, Los Gatos. For tours and special runs, write to P.O. Box 234, Los Gatos, 95030. (408) 395-RIDE. Spring and fall weekends: Sat., 11–5:30; Sun., 12–5:30. In summer: Mon.–Sat., 10:30–4:30; Sun., 11:30–5. Under 2 with an adult, free; others, $1. W.

"Old No. 2," a full-steam narrow-gauge, 18-inch prairie-type locomotive, toots along a mile-long track pulling four open cars. The water tank, a necessity when operating a steam railroad, was designed and built by volunteers, as were the turntable, station, and engine house.

Twenty-nine hand-carved wooden horses and two chariots ride on the 1910 Savage English "roundabout," which turns clockwise, as is the custom in Europe. Five C. W. Parker, two Dare, and two Armitage-Herschel horses have been installed to replace missing horses.

❖ Hidden Villa

26870 Moody Road, Los Altos Hills 94022. (415) 948-4690. Daily except Mon., 9–5:30. Farm tours, summer programs, environmental education programs, and individualized tours, by appt. Call for schedule and prices.

Hidden Villa's 1,600-acre wilderness preserve is relatively unchanged since the days when Ohlone Indians gathered food from its hillsides and took fish from its creeks. A self-guiding tour of the farm area is available, as are four suggested wilderness treks. Visitors can picnic, rent horses, and visit a working vegetable garden, dairy and sheep barn, orchard, and pig and poultry areas. Deanna Fale, who told us about Hidden Villa, wrote, "The preschool tour we took at Hidden Villa was wonderful. The children smelled bay leaves, basil, etc. They held a newly hatched egg. Petted a ewe about to give birth. The guides are knowledgeable and gear their talks to the various age groups. The one-hour tour for four-year-olds was just about right."

❖ Campbell Historical Museum

51 North Central, Campbell 95008. Off First Street and Civic Center Drive. (408) 866-2119. Tues.–Sat., 1:30–4:30. Closed holidays. Donation.

Changing exhibits such as "A Woman's Work Is Never Done," which explores the changes in homemaking in the well-equipped Santa Clara

Valley home from the 1800s to 1900s, reveal the past to help understand the present.

❯❯ Mission Santa Clara de Asis

University of Santa Clara, the Alameda, 820 Alviso, Santa Clara 95053. (408) 984-4242. Daily, 8–5. Free. W.

Founded in 1777 and now part of the university campus, the present mission is a replica of the third building raised on this site by the mission fathers. An adobe wall from the original cloister still stands in the peaceful garden. The original cross of the mission stands in front of the church, and the bell given by the king of Spain in 1778 still tolls.

The **de Saisset Art Museum** (Tues.–Fri., 10–5; weekends, 1–5; 408 544-4545) is on campus and makes an interesting brief stop.

❯❯ Great America

P.O. Box 1776, Santa Clara 95052. On Great America Parkway, off Highway 101. (408) 988-1800. Spring and fall weekends and daily in summer, 10–9; later on Saturdays and holiday weekends. Adults, $21.95; ages 3–6, $10.95; over 55, $14.95. Group rates available. Season passes available at Great America and through BASS/TM outlets. W.

The thrill-ride capital of Northern California offers new experiments in the fast and scary, such as Vortex, the West's only stand-up roller coaster; The Edge, where you fall from a tall tower at 55 miles per hour; Demon, an especially jolting roller coaster; and Grizzly, an old-fashioned wooden roller coaster. At Fort Fun, kids can meet costumed cartoon characters such as Yogi Bear and Fred Flintstone and watch a puppet theater or ride Little Dodge 'Ems, Lady Bugs, and Huck's Hang Gliders. Concerts, a giant screen movie, a bird show, and live stage shows allow for pleasant respites during a day, or night, of adventure.

❯❯ The Recyclery

1601 Dixon Landing Road, Milpitas 95035. (408) 262-1401. Mon.– Sat., 7:30–3:30 for individuals or small groups. Tours for 30–60 people by appt., for third-graders and up. Free.

One of the largest recycling centers in Northern California is spreading the word by showing how it's done. Visitors stand in a glass booth and watch glass, cans, and newspaper being sorted on the floor below. Then the material is hauled by conveyor belts to processing machines, where it is packaged for handling by companies that reuse the materials.

❧ Children's Discovery Museum

*180 Woz Way, San Jose 95110. (408) 298-5437. Tues.–Sat., 10–5;
Sun., 12–5. Adults, $6; ages 4–18 and seniors, $3; members, free. Parking
$2. Theater specials, story telling, and programs. Groups by appt. W.*

The bright-purple, angled Discovery Museum is fun inside and out.
Spectacular hands-on exhibits and games capture the imagination of pre-
and grade-schoolers instantly. Here they can don helmets and climb behind the wheel of a real fire truck. Or slide down a culvert and clamber
through sewer pipes "under the city." They can listen to and talk to traffic
controllers working at the San Jose Airport. The Kids' Bank demystifies
money, and in Waterworks, children pump pedals and spin big screws to
transport water from one level to another. Youngsters can enter an Ohlone
hut, make tortillas and adobe bricks, and do farm chores, while learning
about the layers of history in their world. The Doodad Dump beckons
inventors to glue together infinite varieties of thingamajigs. Creative
physical play, from walking down a "city street" to climbing through a
changing tunnel, is also a winner in the inventive and challenging kids
museum.

❧ The Tech Museum of Innovation

*145 West San Carlos Street, San Jose 95110. (408) 279-7150. Tues.–Sun.,
10–5. Adults, $6; ages 6–18 and seniors, $4; members, free. Hi-tech gift
shop. Groups and evening rentals. W.*

Once called The Garage and the Technology Center, this institution-
in-the-making plans to get young people of all ages excited about technology. Plans are to move The Tech a few blocks away into another new
building created by the architect Legorreta, next to the Children's Discovery Museum. Meanwhile, the challenges are here: The 23-foot-high tower
of 500 telephone books illustrating the amount of information contained
in a molecule of DNA will astound. Astronauts-in-the-making can take
the controls of a Mars Rover model and guide it around the obstacles of a
simulated Martian landscape. Or they can witness the complex interac-
tions that take place on a silicon chip. Young doctors-to-be will be drawn
to the robotics exhibit, which shows how remarkable the human body is.
Exhibits are devoted to the six industries of Silicon Valley: semiconduc-
tors, space, biotechnology, robotics, advanced materials, and bicycles.
Laboratories and a multimedia library draw on the latest technology to
allow visitors to explore on their own.

❖ Rosicrucian Egyptian Museum, Science Museum, and Planetarium

Rosicrucian Park, 1342 Naglee Avenue (at Park), San Jose 95191. (408) 947-3636. Egyptian Museum & Contemporary Art Gallery: daily, 9–5. Adults, $4; seniors and students, $3.50; ages 7–15, $2; under 2, free. Science Center and Planetarium: daily 9–4:15. Science Center: free. Planetarium Shows: adults, $3; seniors and students, $2.50; ages 7–15, $1.50; under 5 not admitted. Call (408) 947-3638 for show times and subjects. Closed Thanksgiving, Christmas, and New Year's Day. Group discounts by reservations. Private planetarium shows and party rentals by arrangement.

The wonderful, faraway world of ancient Egypt awaits to mystify and enchant you in an amazingly large and varied collection. Egyptian and Babylonian mummies, sculpture, paintings, jewelry, cosmetics, scarabs, scrolls, and amulets are here in abundance. The ornate coffins, mummified cats and falcons, and descriptions of the embalming process are totally absorbing—especially to youngsters, who want to know how old everything is. Sumerian clay tablets, a model of the Tower of Babel, a diorama of the Paleolithic period, 25 million years ago, including original tools, and a walk-through Egyptian noble's tomb vie for your attention.

Next door the **Science Center** features the first of the museum's earth science exhibits, "Geological Gems," which includes sections on mineral properties, the quartz family, gemstones, crystals, and rock types. There is also a case of meteorites and a Foucault pendulum on display.

The Rosicrucian Planetarium, a theater of the sky, presents changing programs exploring the myths, mysteries, and facts of the sky of yesterday, today, and tomorrow.

❖ Winchester Mystery House

525 South Winchester Boulevard (between Stevens Creek Boulevard and I-280), San Jose 95128. (408) 247-2101. One-hour tours daily except Christmas, 9:30–4:30 in winter, 9–5:30 in summer. Adults, $12.95; seniors, $9.50; ages 6–12, $6.50. Reduced group tour and catering rates (in Sarah's Cafe) by reservation. Birthday packages available.

Sarah Winchester, widow of the Winchester Rifle heir, was told that as long as she kept building something, she'd never die. So for 38 years, carpenters worked 24 hours a day to build this 160-room mansion filled with mysteries. Doorways open to blank walls, secret passageways twist around, and the number 13 appears everywhere—13-stepped stairways,

13 bathrooms, ceilings with 13 panels, rooms with 13 windows—all in the finest woods and crystals money could buy. Thirteen stately palms line the main driveway.

A self-guided tour of the Victorian Gardens, the Winchester Historical Firearms Museum, and the Antique Products Museum is included in the tour price.

❖ San Jose Historical Museum

1600 Senter Road, San Jose 95112. Kelley Park at Senter Road. (408) 287-2290. Mon.–Fri., 10–4:30; weekends, 12–4:30. Adults, $2; children, $1; seniors, $1.50. Group rates, by appt. Party and picnic facilities. W.

Reconstructed and restored landmarks bring to life the look and feel of late-19th-century San Jose in this 16-acre complex. Walk around the plaza and visit O'Brien's candy store, in 1878 the first place to serve ice cream sodas west of Detroit, the print shop, the 1880s Pacific Hotel, Dashaway stables, the 115-foot electric light tower, the Ng Shing Gung Temple, the Empire firehouse, a 1927 gas station, Coyote post office, Steven's Ranch fruit barn, H. H. Warburton's doctor's office, the 1909 Bank of Italy building, and the many Victorian homes that have been saved and moved to museum premises. Poet Edwin Markham's Greek Revival home is being restored. Our favorite is the little Umbarger House, a delicious 1870s gingerbread confection that has been completely furnished, right down to the clothes in the closets and the dishes in the sink.

❖ Japanese Friendship Tea Garden

1300 Senter Road, Kelley Park, San Jose 95112. (408) 277-5254. Daily, 10–sunset. Free.

This tranquil garden is patterned after the Korakuen garden in San Jose's sister city of Okayama. The three lakes are designed to symbolize the word *kokoro*, which means "heart-mind-and-soul." Picturesque bridges and waterfalls, shaped rocks and trees, and land and water flowers are wonderful to wander around. Naturally, the children will head over to watch the families of *koi*, fat gold, white, or black carp who come when dinner is offered.

❖ Happy Hollow Park and Zoo

1300 Senter Road, Kelley Park, San Jose 95112. (408) 292-8188. Open daily; call for hours and fees. Advance group reservations available. Parking fee, $3. W.

Enjoy Danny the Dragon as he prowls through a bamboo forest, and listen as a chorus of sea animals invites you to enter King Neptune's kingdom. Climb a stairway in the Crooked House and slide down a spiral slide. Visit the many play areas dotting the park, and view a puppet show at the puppet castle theatre. The zoo offers youngsters a chance to see exotic animals from all over the world. They can cuddle a baby goat or pet a baby llama.

❖ Youth Science Institute—Vasona Discovery Center

296 Garden Hill Drive, Los Gatos 95030. Vasona County Park, off Blossom Hill Road. (408) 356-4945. Mon.–Fri., 9–4:30; Parking fee, $3. Picnic facilities.

The Vasona Discovery Center is a junior museum featuring exhibits of aquatic life and dinosaurs. Live animals on display include fish, reptiles, and amphibians. School and community children's science classes are taught at the center.

❖ Youth Science Institute—Sanborn Discovery Center

16055 Sanborn Road, Saratoga 95070. Sanborn-Skyline County Park, off Highway 9. (408) 867-6940. Weekends, 9–4; weekdays, by appt. Parking fee, $3. Picnic tables and hiking trails.

The Sanborn Discovery Center, located in a redwood forest, is a junior museum with a live insect zoo and other live animals on display including rattlesnakes, turtles, chinchillas, and a variety of fish, reptiles, and amphibians. School and community children's science classes are taught at the center.

❖ Youth Science Institute—Alum Rock Discovery Center

16260 Alum Rock Avenue, San Jose 95127. Alum Rock Park, off Highway 680. (408) 258-4322. Tues.–Fri., 9–4:30; Sat., 12–4:30; Sun. between Easter and Labor Day, 10:30–4:30. Closed Sun. and Mon. in winter. Adults, 50 cents; children, 25 cents. Parking fee, $3.

The Alum Rock Discovery Center is a junior museum with an extensive collection of live animals, reptiles, amphibians, and birds (including hawks and owls). Bird species are displayed. There is a resource library, and several activities are always in the works. Alum Rock Park has trails, streams, and picnic facilities.

❖ New Almaden Quicksilver Mining Museum

21570 Almaden Road (P.O. Box 124), New Almaden 95042. (408) 268-1729. Sat., 12–4. Donation.

Until the County Park Association opens its new museum on the site of the old mine office in the hacienda furnace yard, the "Original New

Almaden Mercury Mining Museum" and the mining artifacts gathered by Constance Perham, who as a young girl accompanied her father on trips to the mines, serves as a fascinating reminder of the early settlers.

❧ Flying Lady II Restaurant and Wagons to Wings Museum

15060 Foothill Road, Morgan Hill 95037. (408) 779-4136/227-4607. Lunch and dinner, Wed.–Sun.; Sun., Dixieland Jazz Brunch. Moderate prices. Museum open Wed.–Sun., 10–8. Free.

One of the world's largest restaurants, the Flying Lady II is an adventure in dining. Seven full-sized antique aircraft hang over the spectacular main dining room along with over 100 scale model airplanes "flying" over diners on a moving track. Antique flags of the world and merry-go-round horses add to the colorful atmosphere.

The Wagons to Wings Museum is home to antique cars, aircraft, and horse-drawn wagons, including the 1929 Fort Tri-Motor seen in the movie *Indiana Jones and the Temple of Doom.*

❧ Gilroy Historical Museum

195 Fifth Street (at Church), Gilroy 95020. (408) 848-0470. Mon.–Fri., 9–5; irregularly on Sat. Closed holidays. Donation.

Telephones, tools, and toys are just part of this collection of over 22,000 donated memories from Gilroy's pioneer families. A cigar-store Indian, a school desk, and Ohlone clothing and artifacts are kids' favorites. Rotating exhibits emphasize the tobacco industry that was important in the building of the town, which once was home to the world's largest cigar factory, and to Henry Miller, the local cattle king.

❧ Lick Observatory

Mt. Hamilton 95140. Highway 130, 25 miles Southeast of San Jose. (408) 274-5061. Gallery, 10–5 daily; tours, 1:30–4:30. Closed holidays. Gift store. Free.

A long, narrow, winding road takes you to the top of Mt. Hamilton and the awesome domes of Lick Observatory. It was here that four of the satellites of Jupiter were discovered—the first since the time of Galileo. Now star clusters and galaxies are studied with the most modern equipment. The visitor's gallery looks up at one of the largest telescopes (120 inches) in the world, a Shane reflecting telescope, and the tour of photos and astronomical instruments is intriguing and educational. The gallery is half a mile from the Visitor Center. Star gazing is possible for the public on summer Fridays, but you must write, enclosing a self-addressed, stamped envelope for one to six tickets, to Visitors Program, Lick Observatory, Mt. Hamilton 95140. Remember that there are no food or gas facilities nearby.

≫ Public Relations Tours

Acres of Orchids. Rod McLellan Orchidary. 1450 El Camino Real, South San Francisco 94080. (415) 871-5655. Open 10–5; guided tours, 10:30 and 1:30 daily. Free. Orchids in more colors, types, and sizes than you can imagine are here for looking, smelling, and buying.

U.S. Weather Service. Bayshore Freeway, San Bruno. San Francisco International Airport. (415) 876-2886. See the materials used in briefing pilots and the weather teletypes and instruments. Free tours, by appointment, for fourth-graders and up. The facility plans to move to Monterey, so call for information.

Sunset Magazine. Middlefield and Willow roads, Menlo Park 94025-3691. One mile west of Highway 101. (415) 321-3600. Guided tours, Mon.–Fri. at 10:30 and 2:30. Groups by appointment. Gardens open 8–4:30.

Budding journalists can see the editorial offices, test kitchens, patios, and office entertainment areas, and the test and formal gardens. During the holidays they can view decorations and crafts designed and executed by the staff. They can also enjoy the Sunset gardens: when you walk on a path from one end to the other, you view, in geographic sequence, the botanical life of the Western coast of America—from Northwest rhododendrons and azaleas to the cactus of the desert.

HEADING SOUTH BY THE SEA

 THE SANTA CRUZ AREA

The Santa Cruz area is small, nestled on a bay southwest of San Jose and north of Monterey. Big Basin Redwoods, Natural Bridges, and Loch Lomond parks are some of the natural sites of interest, and, along with Castroville, home of the artichoke, are perfect day trips.

Here you can find birdwatching, butterfly watching, whale watching, and herb and heritage walks, as well as sky and sea walks. In Santa Cruz, beaches are the main attraction. If you're coming from San Francisco, be sure to bring along car games to while away the two-hour ride. Highway 1, along the coast, is more beautiful and easier to drive than the faster choice, Highways 101 and 17.

⤜ Roaring Camp & Big Trees Narrow-Gauge Railroad and Santa Cruz, Big Trees & Pacific Railway Company

P.O. Box G-1, Felton 95018. Take Highway 17 to the Mt. Hermon Road exit in Scotts Valley, then drive west 3.5 miles to the end of the road at Felton, and left onto Graham Hill Road. (408) 335-4400. Roaring Camp round-trip fares: ages 3–15, $8; over 16, $11. Santa Cruz, Big Trees round-trip: $8.95 and $12.95. Group rates available. Call for schedules.

Old-time train buffs now have two fabulous train rides to choose from, both originating at Roaring Camp. Great steam locomotives hiss and puff through the redwoods on the steepest narrow-gauge railroad grade in North America and around the tightest turns to the top of Big Mountain. The 1 1/4 hour trip transports riders back 100 years.

On the two-hour "Picnic Line" between Roaring Camp and the Santa Cruz beaches, passengers ride in historic 1902 wooden and 1926 steel passenger cars and open vista cars pulled by steam and early diesel loco-motives, round trip and one way. Back in Roaring Camp, you can explore an 1880s logging town, wander along nature trails, rest beside an 1840s covered bridge, chow down at the Chuck Wagon Bar-B-Cue, and on sum-mer weekends, enjoy Country Western music.

❧ Lighthouse Surfing Museum

*West Cliff Drive, Santa Cruz 95060. (408) 429-3760. Mon.–Fri., 12–4;
in summer, also Sat. and Sun. until 5. Free.*

The Santa Cruz Surfing Museum, the only surfing museum on the
planet, is located in the Mark Abbott Memorial Lighthouse on Lighthouse
Point overlooking "steamer's lane," the best surfboard inlet in the area.
On display are photographs, surfboards, and other surfing memorabilia
tracing more than 50 years of surfing in the Santa Cruz area.

❧ Long Marine Laboratory & Aquarium

*Off Delaware Avenue, near Natural Bridges State Park, Santa Cruz 95060.
(408) 426-4308. Tues., 1–4. Group tours by appt.*

A marine research facility of the University of California at Santa
Cruz, this is a working laboratory featuring fascinating tide pool aquariums, touch tanks, the skeleton of an 85-foot blue whale, a dolphinarium,
and a glimpse of current research. Tide-pool exploration tours are also
available.

❧ The Mystery Spot

*1953 Banciforte Drive, Santa Cruz 95065. (408) 423-8897. Daily, 9–5.
Adults, $3; under 11, $1.50. Tours and group rates.*

All the laws of gravity are challenged in this scary natural curiosity.
Balls roll uphill, the trees can't stand up straight, and you always seem to
be standing either backwards or sideways. One test here is to lay a
carpenter's level across two cement blocks, checking to see that their tops
are on the same level. Then stand on one and see your friend on the other
suddenly shrink or grow tall. You can also walk up the walls of a cabin
that looks cockeyed, but isn't. Alice-in-Wonderland's caterpillar would
feel right at home.

❧ Santa Cruz Beach and Boardwalk

*400 Beach Street (at Riverside Avenue), Santa Cruz 95060. (408) 423-
5590. Opens at 11, daily; until 5 in winter and until 11, Memorial Day to
Labor Day, depending on the weather. Open weekends and holidays (except
Christmas) throughout the year. Package tickets for 50 individual rides,
$19.95; for all day, $16.95. Individual ride tickets and group rates
available. Reservations for groups. General admission is free. Free off-site
picnic tables. Free wheelchairs to borrow. Bike locks, $5 a day. Birthday
parties with Captain Nemo by appt. W.*

The Giant Dipper, one of the world's ten top roller coasters, and the
classic 1911 Looff merry-go-round, with 72 hand-carved wooden horses,
are both magnets for kids at California's only remaining amusement park

on the beach. The last of the old-time West Coast boardwalks, Santa Cruz has everything you hope to find on one: a Ferris wheel, bumper cars, skee-ball, a penny-video arcade, miniature golf, cotton candy, sweet and scary rides—including the new Hurricane roller coaster and the Wave Jammer. The Neptune's Kingdom entertainment complex is a two-story treasure island of fun, with theme miniature golf, family pool tables, air hockey, and "foos ball," as well as a state-of-the-art video complex and a display of historical photos. There are 19 restaurants and fast-food vendors on the boardwalk, and the best thing of all, a wonderful white beach, with para-sailing and kayaking facilities.

On the pier nearby, you can fish and see sea lions swimming around the pilings.

❯ Santa Cruz City Museum

1305 East Cliff Drive (at Pilkington), Santa Cruz 95062. (408) 429-3773. Tues.–Sat., 10–5; Sun, 12–5. Donation. Reserved parking on Pilkington in summer.

A "gray whale" welcomes you to natural history exhibits of animals, birds, and local plant groups. Learn how local Ohlone Indians lived; grind acorns in a stone mortar. See a mastodon skull from a prehistoric denizen of the region. Touch live tide-pool animals. You can picnic in the park that surrounds the museum, or build a sand castle on the beach across the street. A slide show on the geology of Santa Cruz is played on request. Seasonal group tours by appointment.

The kids will be right at home in the **Children's Art Foundation** (915 Cedar Street 95060; 408 426-5557), which collects, preserves, and exhibits children's art from around the world, publishes *Stone Soup*, a magazine of writing and art by children, and gives art lessons. Open Monday through Friday, 1 to 5:30 and by appointment, free.

❯ William H. Volck Memorial Museum

261 East Beach Street, Watsonville 95060. (408) 722-0305. Tues.–Thurs., 11–3, and by appt. Free.

Local history is lovingly preserved in this community museum featuring items and artifacts from the Pajaro Valley. We like the fine collection of historic costumes and textiles, from gingham sunbonnets and aprons to opera hats and ball gowns.

❯ Elkhorn Slough National Estuarine Research Reserve

1700 Elkhorn Road, Watsonville 95076. (408) 728-2822. Wed.–Sun., 9–5; Sat. and Sun., walks at 10 and 1, talk 2–3. Visitors Center, free.

Walks, $2.50 for those over 16, free for those with valid fishing/hunting license. Gift shop. W.

Videos are shown and special events take place in the visitors center, run by the California Wildlands Program, which has displays of the natural history surrounding it. Blooming plants are identified. There are several guided nature trails.

In spring, the wildflowers are rampant. In summer, small leopard sharks and smooth hound sharks come in on the high tide to feed on crabs and clams. Migrating shorebirds attract visitors in the fall. And in winter, hawks nest.

Public Relations Tours

Salz Tannery Tour. 1040 River Street, Santa Cruz 95060. (408) 423-1480. Free. Tours by appointment for groups of 8 to 25. The oldest tannery west of Chicago, Salz produces fine leather goods and accessories.

THE MONTEREY AREA

Since its discovery in 1542 by Spanish explorer Juan Cabrillo, the Monterey Peninsula has been a mecca for vagabonds and visionaries, pioneers in agriculture and art. It was here that California, after being under the flags of Spain and Mexico, was made part of the United States.

The Monterey area offers many things worth investigating: the state's best-preserved and -presented tribute to its early history in Monterey; a magnificent coastline in Big Sur; Salinas, with its reminders of novelist John Steinbeck; a sweeping windswept valley now turning into fertile farmland; Pinnacles National Monument; and the San Antonio de Padua Mission. From San Francisco, allow three hours driving time on Highway 101, taking the Monterey turnoff, or three and a half hours by the prettier coast route.

San Juan Bautista State Historic Park

P.O. Box 1110, San Juan Bautista 95045-1110. Take Highway 156 exit off Highway 101. (408) 623-4881. Daily, 10–4:30 in winter, until 5 in summer. Adults, $2; children, $1. Separate donation for the mission. Tours by appt. Check at Ranger Station for scheduled interpretive activities. Call for information on Living History Days, when volunteers don period costumes and reenact events from California's past.

A mission, a museum, an adobe house, an 1870s hotel and stables, a wash house, blacksmith shop, granary, and cabin all encircle the lovely plaza of San Juan Bautista, representing three periods in California history—Spanish, Mexican, and early Californian.

Start your visit at the **Mission of San Juan Bautista**, founded in 1797 and carefully preserved. The old adobe rooms house many treasures, including a 1737 barrel organ, gaming sticks of the San Juan Indians, and artifacts from the original building. The original bells still call parishioners to mass. In the mission gardens, today's youngsters can learn some of the same things the Indians were taught: weaving, candlemaking, and baking.

Cross to the **Castro Adobe**, which also houses General Castro's secretary's office. This should serve as a model for other museums: Every room is completely labeled, with pictures to aid in the identification of the objects. The house is furnished as it was in the 1870s by the Breen family, who survived the Donner Party disaster to find a fortune in the gold fields. You'll see the candlesticks that came west with the Breens and the diary, wardrobe, gloves, fan, and card case of Isabella Breen. The kitchen is complete, right down to the boot pull.

The Plaza Hotel, next door, is noted for its barroom with billiard and poker tables standing ready. Built in 1813 as a barracks for the Spanish soldiers, its walls now display Wells Fargo memorabilia and photos of the pioneers, and a slide show brings "the early years" to life.

Diagonally across the plaza is the **Zanetta House**, a completely furnished Victorian home, with dishes on the table and singing bird in the parlor, built on the foundation of the adobe that once housed the Indian maidens of the settlement. The **Livery Stable** is jammed with wonderful wagons including a surrey with a fringe on top, an Amish buggy by Studebaker, a "tally ho wagon," phaetons, and buckboards.

The streets nearby have interesting shops and restaurants, making San Juan Bautista a perfect place to spend a relaxing morning or afternoon.

❖ San Luis Reservoir

Romero Overlook. Highway 152, 15 miles west of Los Banos. (209) 826-1196. Daily, 9–5. Closed major holidays. Free.

In the Romero Overlook on the reservoir, pictures, graphic wall displays, movies, and slide shows tell the story of the State Water Project and the Federal Central Valley Project, and how they work together at the San Luis Complex. Telescopes at the center offer a spectacular view of the area. State Water Resources guides staff the Visitors Center.

❖ Monterey

In this bustling town, The Path of History, natural attractions, and busy shops lure visitors. Fisherman's Wharf is a melange of restaurants, fish stores, and shops, and although seal watching is the favored pastime, you can go for a boat ride or take a diving bell 30 feet down to look at the ocean's floor. There are also picnic tables near the bocce ball courts. In Monterey, you can go hang-gliding, ballooning, tide-pooling, and on nature walks.

Today's Cannery Row is a far cry from the Cannery Row in John Steinbeck's books. Now it is a growing complex of restaurants, shops, and galleries offering entertainment for all. Its greatest attraction is the extraordinary Monterey Bay Aquarium.

The City of Monterey has made it easy for visitors to see its beginnings. By following the yellow line painted on several streets, you follow **"The Path of History."** Landmark plaques tell briefly who built historic houses, and why they're landmarks. Six of the houses along The Path of History are also part of the **Monterey State Historic Park** complex, and day tickets to the park will admit you to all six adobes in MSHP (described below: Larkin House, Stevenson House, Cooper-Molera, Casa Sobranes, Custom House, and Pacific House). Day tickets are $3.50 for adults, $2 for children, or you can pay $2 per building, $1 per building for children. Call to arrange group tours. All are closed on Christmas, New Year's, and Thanksgiving.

❖ The Larkin House

510 Calle Principal (at Jefferson Street), Monterey 93940. (408) 649-7118. Guided tours on the hour, 10–4, daily except Tues.

Built by Thomas Oliver Larkin, the first and only U.S. consul to Mexico stationed in Monterey, the house is an architectural and historical gem. It was the first home in Monterey in the New England style, with two stories, as well as the first to have glass windows. Many of the furnishings are original. Through the rose-covered garden is a small house, now a museum, used in 1847–49 by Civil War general William Tecumseh Sherman, then an Army lieutenant. It's said that he left a beautiful woman waiting in vain for his return.

❖ The Stevenson House

Houston Street, Monterey 93940. (408) 649-7118. Tours on the hour, 10–4 daily except Wed. W (first floor only). Nov. 13 is an open house for RLS's "unbirthday" because he gave it away. Special events and school programs.

In 1879 Robert Louis Stevenson spent a few months in a second-floor room of this boardinghouse. He had traveled from Scotland to visit Fanny Osbourne, who later became his wife. He wrote *The Old Pacific Capital* here. The house is restored to look as it did then, with several rooms devoted to Stevenson memorabilia. Be sure to see the doll collection upstairs. There is a rumor of a ghost.

After a visit, third-grader Jennifer wrote, "Thank you for a fun day at the 'French Hotel.' I like Robert Stevenson. I like looking inside his room. I learned that Stevenson gave his birthday to a little girl named Annie. Thank you for the cake."

❧ Cooper-Molera Adobe

Polk and Munras streets, Monterey 93940. (408) 649-7118. Tours on the hour, 10–4 daily except Wed.

This restored complex contains Captain John Cooper's townhouse (his wife was Mariano Vallejo's sister Encarnacion), several adobe buildings, period gardens with scratching chickens, and a museum store.

❧ Casa Sobranes

336 Pacific Street (at Del Monte), Monterey 93940. (408) 649-7118. Tours on the hour, 10–4 daily except Tues. and Thurs.

"The House with the Blue Gate" is an authentic, typical home of Mexican California. The furnishings reflect the blend of early New England and China trade pieces with Mexican folk art. A collection of local art graces the house as well.

❧ The Custom House

1 Custom House Plaza, Monterey 93940. (408) 649-7118. Daily, 10–4; until 5 in summer.

The United States flag was first officially raised in California over this building, in 1846. It is here that each ship captain presented his cargo for the customs inspector. Today, you walk into a long room that holds the cargo Richard Henry Dana wrote about in his novel *Two Years Before the Mast*. There are casks of liquor, cases of dishes, bags of nails, coffee, and flour, and wagon wheels. A screeching yellow and green parrot rules a roost of ribbons, ropes, cloth, shawls, soap, paper, tools, and trunks. In one area, piles of "California bank notes"—cowhides—wait to be used for trading. The Custom House manager's quarters upstairs feature a carved bed and chest, a table, and a desk with an open ledger.

❖ Pacific House

10 Custom House Plaza, Monterey 93940. (408) 649-7118. Daily, 10–4; until 5 in summer.

The first floor of this tavern-court-newspaper-church-ballroom is now a museum of California history, with artifact-filled cases arranged chronologically. From the Costanoan Indian artifacts to Spanish saddles and money, gold miners' tools, a whaling boat, and then the Victorian furniture of the pioneers, a historical array is presented, unfolding like a storybook. Upstairs is the Holman Collection, a remarkable gathering of Indian relics from all over North America. Costanoan religion, hunting, fishing, gathering and processing of acorns, housing, trade, transportation, warfare, and survival lessons are explained with artifacts and models. Compare the arrows, games, beads, and baskets of many tribes, from Alaskan Eskimos to American Indians.

❖ Sancho Panza Restaurant

Casa Gutierrez, 590 Calle Principal, Monterey 93940. (408) 375-0095. Daily, 11–2 and 5–9; later in summer.

Built in 1841 by a young Mexican for his bride, the old adobe is now a comfortable Mexican inn that feels like an early Monterey home. The father earned his living as a farmer and rancher, and raised 15 children here. Today, Casa Gutierrez is part of the Monterey State Historic Park, 42 historic adobe buildings found along The Path of History. A warm fire blazes on cool evenings, and there's a garden in back for lunch and summer nights. Prices are reasonable and the food is delicious. Tortilla- and tamale-making demonstrations are scheduled with park rangers.

❖ The Boston Store

Corner of Scott and Olivier streets, Monterey 93940. (408) 649-3364. Wed.–Sat., 10–5; 12–5 on Sun. Free.

Built by Thomas O. Larkin about 1845, this structure housed a general merchandise store operated by Joseph Boston and Company in the 1850s. The building was later called Casa del Oro because it was supposed to have served as a gold depository. Today, it is again a general merchandise store, operated by the Monterey History & Art Association and staffed by docents.

❖ Monterey's First Theatre/Jack Swan's Tavern

Corner of Scott and Pacific streets, Monterey 93940. Building information: (408) 375-5100. Theater information: (408) 375-4916. Fri. and Sat., 1–8; Wed. and Thurs., 1–5. Free.

Jack Swan's lodging house gave its first performance of a stage play in 1847 to entertain bored soldiers. Since then theatrical productions have been produced regularly, and now 19th-century melodramas are performed on weekends. During the day you can walk through and look at the theatrical memorabilia, including a playbill for Lola Montez. The theater company celebrated its 50th anniversary in 1987.

❖ Allen Knight Maritime Museum

5 Custom House Plaza, Monterey 93940. (408) 375-2553. Memorial Day–Labor Day, 10–8 daily except Mon.; in winter, 10–5 daily except Mon. Groups by appt. Donation. W.

A spiffy new building captures the maritime tradition of Monterey. Fans will recognize the captain's cabin from an old sailing ship, with bed, writing desk, the sardine boat, and the sailor's ditty box. They'll also find the Fresnel lens from the lighthouse at Point Sur on a turnable turntable, as well as models, photos, lithographs, paintings, and various old sailing accoutrements: octants, ships' bells, sailors' thimbles, Arctic goggles, scrimshaw, and ships' logs in the seven galleries. A small theater shows films of state history. Special sea chanty sessions, story-telling events, and other programs will bring kids back for more.

❖ Colton Hall Museum of the City of Monterey

Pacific Street (between Jefferson and Madison), Monterey 93940. (408) 375-9944. Daily, 10–5. Free.

Colton Hall, the first town hall and public school of Monterey, was the site of the first Constitutional Convention of the State of California, in 1849. Here the California Constitution was written in Spanish and English and the Great Seal of the state was designed. The large meeting room is furnished as it was then, with displays depicting the scene in 1849 during the convention, as if the delegates had just stepped out for a break.

Behind Colton Hall is the **Old Monterey Jail**, open daily until 5. The walls are granite, two feet thick, the doors are iron, and the cells tell the stories of the jail and its inmates. Believe it or not, this was the city jail until 1959. In John Steinbeck's *Tortilla Flat*, for Danny, the Old Monterey Jail was a second home.

❖ Spirit of Monterey Steinbeck Wax Museum

700 Cannery Row, Monterey 93940-1085. (408) 375-3770. Daily, 11– 8, longer hours in summer. Adults, $4.95; ages 6–16, $2.95; over 65, $3.95. Tours with special rates by appt. W.

Dozens of scenes tell the spellbinding story of Monterey and the people who lived it, from the Indians who lived here before the Spanish galleons cast anchor to Steinbeck's rowdy crew. Here visitors meet Conception, who fell in love with a Russian officer and waited in vain for his return; Robert Louis Stevenson; the Spanish dons who ruled Monterey; and Thomas Larkin, who was California's first "ambassador" to the United States, among other roles. Kit Carson rides up and tells his story, Joaquin Murietta spouts poetry, and Steinbeck reminisces about his friends in the Lone Star Cafe.

❖ Monterey Bay Aquarium
886 Cannery Row, Monterey 93940-1085. (408) 648-4888. Advance purchase: (800) 756-3737. Daily, except Christmas, 10–6. Adults, $9.75; students and seniors, $7.25; ages 3–12, $4.50. Posted feeding schedules. Regularly scheduled workshops and discovery labs. Group rates and tours available.

"He's feeding fish to fish," one youngster exclaimed, while standing entranced before the three-story kelp forest. All the wonders of a hidden world come to light at the internationally acclaimed Monterey Bay Aquarium, one of California's "top 11" attractions. In a startling undersea tour of Monterey Bay, visitors will meet 525 living species in 23 habitat galleries and exhibits. California sea otters frolic nose to nose with you in their own naturalistic pool, visible on two different levels. You can investigate with telescopes and microscopes, play with bat rays and starfish, or walk through a shorebird aviary. Did you know that one animal is the deadliest in the ocean and also is a popular snack, and that it can be a quarter of an inch across—or longer than 100 feet? "The Planet of the Jellies," a year-long exhibit, shows over a dozen beautiful species, some trailing lacy tentacles, others pulsing with rainbow bands of light.

Twice a week, "Live from the Deep Canyon" lets visitors peek over the shoulders of scientists in a research submarine and look at unusual creatures living 3,000 feet and more below the surface of Monterey Bay.

Films, slide shows, special programs, and hands-on interpretive exhibits challenge and intrigue. The aquarium is outstanding, a beautifully designed treat for the whole family.

❖ Dennis the Menace Playground
El Estero City Park (off Del Monte Avenue), Camino del Estero and Fremont, Monterey 93941. Open during daylight hours. Free.

Youngsters will want to head to this colorful playspace designed by cartoonist Hank Ketchum. Here little potential "menaces" can let off steam in a steam switch engine, hang from the Umbrella Tree, sweep down the Giant Swing Ride, and put their heads in the lion's mouth for a drink of water.

❖ U.S. Army Museum

The Presidio, Monterey 93944. (408) 647-5119/242-8414. Thur.–Mon., 9–12:30 and 1:30–4. Free. The Presidio is scheduled for closure, and the museum will then close as well, so do call first.

This Army-run museum displays the history of old Fort Hill from the Ohlone Indian period to the present. Monuments to Commander John Drake Sloat and Father Junipero Serra adjoin the museum. Ten history sites are located nearby, including Rumsen village sites and ceremonial rock, Father Serra's landing place, and the ruins of the first American fort in Monterey. The museum collection includes uniforms from the turn of the century, saddles, swords, sabers, and other Army equipment, and dioramas of early forts and the first Presidio.

❖ Pacific Grove Museum of Natural History

Forest and Central avenues, Pacific Grove 93950. (408) 648-3116. Daily except Mon., 10–5. Closed major holidays. Groups by appt. Free. W.

Each October, thousands of Monarch butterflies arrive in Pacific Grove to winter in a grove of pine trees until March. Visitors who arrive in other months can see a marvelous exhibit of the Monarch in this beautifully designed museum. There is also a large collection of tropical and other California butterflies as well as sea otters, fish, mammals, rodents, insects, and birds, stuffed and in photos. The skeleton of a sea otter playing with a clamshell is touching. The life of the Costanoan Indian is revealed in an archaeological "dig."

Dioramas and the amazing relief map of Monterey Bay are also worth a look—if the youngsters can tear themselves away from the whale in front. Films also are shown.

❖ Point Piños Lighthouse

Off Seventeen-Mile Drive, Pacific Grove 93950. Information at Pacific Grove Museum: (408) 648-3116. Weekends, 1–4. Free.

The oldest working lighthouse (1855) on the West Coast, Point Piños, Point of Pines, was named by explorer Sebastian Viscaino in 1602. It overlooks the meadows and sand dunes of a golf course on one side, and the whitecapped ocean on the other. A small U.S. Coast Guard maritime museum is open to the public.

The short distance to town along scenic Oceanview Boulevard offers many beautiful sights. Along the way you'll pass Lovers Point, with marine gardens, and tree-shaded picnic grounds.

☞ Carmel Mission, Mission San Carlos Borromeo

Rio Road (off Highway 1), Carmel 93923. (408) 624-1271. Daily except holidays, 9:30–4:30. Donation.

The lovely mission church and cemetery, three museums, and the adobe home of the pioneer Munras family combine to make this mission a "must stop." Father Junipero Serra rests in the church, and in the cemetery lies Old Gabriel, 119 years old, baptized by Father Serra. A small museum in the garden houses pictures of the original mission and its restoration. There are Indian grinding pots, arrowheads, baskets, beads, and toys. The long main museum offers fine art from the original mission and a replica of the stark cell Father Serra died in. You'll also find California's first library here—Father Serra's books, bibles, travel commentaries, and technical works. Altar pieces, saddles, the furnished kitchen and dining room, a "clacker" used instead of bells, and a fabulous new nativity crèche are also of interest, as are mementos of Pope Paul's visit in 1987.

Casa Munras is now a memorial to the Munras family. Visitors can see the keys from the original adobe, family pictures, music and provision boxes, a doctor's bag, jewelry, dresses, and a totally furnished living room.

☞ Carmel

A visit to the Monterey Peninsula is not complete without an hour or two of browsing in the picturesque village of Carmel. The Pine Inn Block, bounded by Ocean Avenue, Lincoln, Monte Verde, and Sixth Avenue, is bustling with Victorian shops, gardens, and restaurants. The Mediterranean Market at Ocean and Mission (408 624-2022) supplies picnic goodies for your walk on Carmel Beach, at the end of Ocean Avenue.

☞ Tor House

26304 Ocean View Avenue, Carmel 93923. (408) 624-1813. One-hour tours on Fri. and Sat. by reservation: 624-1840. Adults, $5; $3.50 for college students, $1.50 for high school students.

Mature, budding poets over 12 years old will enjoy a visit to the home of California poet Robinson Jeffers on a high bluff overlooking the Pacific. Part English country cottage, part stone monument to the mystery of the human imagination, Tor House celebrates the nature around it. Jeffers himself built the low main cottage of "stone love stone," with memorabilia from his world travels imbedded in the stone walls, and the 40-foot Hawk Tower that looks like a castle turret. He also built a wonderful "dungeon playroom" for his sons.

❖ Point Lobos State Reserve

Box 62, Carmel 93923. Highway 1, south of Carmel. (408) 624-4909. Daily, 9–5 in winter, later in summer. Cars, $6; $5 for senior citizens.

Early Spanish explorers named this rocky, surf-swept point of land *Punta de Los Lobos Marinos*, or Point of the Sea Wolves. You can still hear the loud barking of the sea lions and see them on offshore rocks. Point Lobos is an outdoor museum: Each tree, plant, and shrub is protected by law, as are the cormorants, pelicans, otters, squirrels, and black-tailed mule deer that live here. One of the last natural stands of Monterey cypress is also found at the reserve. Picnic areas and hiking trails abound. Dogs are not permitted in the reserve.

❖ Thunderbird Book Shop & Restaurant & Thunderbird for Kids

The Barnyard, P.O. Box 22830, Carmel 93922. Off Highway 1 and Carmel Valley Road. (408) 624-4995. Daily, 10–6; Thurs. to Sat., until 9.

The Thunderbird is just what you dream a bookstore might be—a place where browsing is welcomed and the selection of books is extensive. One corner of the store is an informal restaurant. And you can keep browsing as you nosh. Thunderbird for Kids is devoted to the creativity of children. It offers children's entertainment, parenting workshops, toys, science and art supplies, and the Great Little Book Club.

❖ The Steinbeck House

132 Central Avenue, Salinas. Reservations: (408) 424-2735. Seatings at 11:45 or 1:15, Mon.–Fri. Gift shop.

John Steinbeck's childhood Victorian home is now a luncheon restaurant offering fresh produce of the valley amid Steinbeck memorabilia. This is where Steinbeck wrote *The Red Pony* and *Tortilla Flat*. The "Best Cellar" features Steinbeck's books. Profits go to Salinas Valley charities and the house's restoration has been funded by the luncheon proceeds.

The Steinbeck Library at 110 West San Luis (408 758-7311) displays an extensive collection of John Steinbeck's memorabilia, including reviews and personal correspondence and a life-size bronze statue.

❖ The First Mayor's House

238 East Romie Lane, Salinas 93901. (408) 757-8085. First Sun. of the month, 1–4. Free.

Built in 1868 by Isaac Harvey, the first mayor of Salinas, of redwood lumber hauled from Moss Landing, the cottage has been moved to its present location. The Monterey County Historical Society is continuing to work on its restoration.

◈ The Boronda Adobe

Boronda Road at West Laurel Drive, Salinas 93901. (408) 757-8085. Weekends, 1–4; and by appt. Free.

The Monterey County Historical Society has also restored Jose Eusebio Boronda's unaltered rancho, built in 1844. It's now a museum proudly showing many of its original furnishings.

◈ Issei Pioneer Museum

14 California Street, Salinas 93901. (408) 424-4105. By appt. Free.

The first and only *Issei* pioneer museum in the United States, housed in the annex of a Buddhist temple, contains over 600 items related to the Issei—the first generation of Japanese to emigrate to the United States, in the 1890s and early 1900s. The museum was opened in 1976, the bicentennial year of our country. Many of the articles were handmade by the Issei during World War II in various relocation camps. The oldest item is a book about Tokyo, printed in 1850. The museum also houses many items of historical significance collected by Y. Takemura.

◈ Mission Nuestra Señora de la Soledad

36641 Fort Romie Road, Soledad 93960. Highway 101 southwest of Soledad. Arroyo Seco off-ramp, then right on Fort Romie Road. (408) 678-2586. Daily except Tues., 10–4.

Founded in 1791 as the 13th in the chain of 21 California missions, this mission dedicated to Holy Mary, Our Lady of the Solitude, was in desolate open plains and in ruins by 1859. Volunteers have restored it as a lovely oasis surrounded by gardens. Visitors may visit the museum and chapel and then spend time in the gift shop, graveyard, and picnic area.

◈ San Antonio de Padua Mission

P.O. Box 803, Jolon 93928. On Fort Hunter Liggett, off Highway 101 from King City or Bradley. (408) 385-4478. Mon.–Sat., 9:30–4:30; Sun., 11–5, mass at 10 A.M. Donation. Information for fourth-graders may be obtained by a request accompanied by a S.A.S.E.

San Antonio de Padua is one of the finest of the missions. It was the third mission founded by Fra Junipero Serra, in 1771. A military base around it has preserved its natural setting, and to visit it is to feel that you're discovering the days of the padres and Salinan Indians of 200 years ago. Inside the mission museum, on a self-guided tour, you'll see artifacts from mission days, tools for candle-making and carpentry, the old wine press, and other old-time implements needed to run a working mission. The grist mill, the aqueduct system, waterwheel, and wine vat stand as the Indians saw them when San Antonio was at its height. The wildflower season in late April and early May is gorgeous, and the annual Fiesta Bar-B-Q is held on the second Sunday of June, close to the Feast of St. Anthony. Steinbeck described the mission in a state of abandonment in *To a God Unknown*. Today it is a working parish and contemplative center and retreat, served by the Franciscan Friars of California.

❧ Public Relations Tours

Roses of Yesterday and Today. 803 Browns Valley Road, Watsonville 95076. (408) 724-3537. Tours by appt. The big rose garden that specializes in old, hard-to-find roses is, in season, a sight to behold.

Stone Container Corporation. 1078 Merrill Street, Salinas 93901. (408) 414-1831. Nov.–Apr., by appt., for children over 10. Visitors see the manufacture of corrugated boxes and paper laminations. Free.

The Herald Newspaper. 8 Upper Ragsdale Drive (P.O. Box 271), Monterey 93942. (408) 648-1192. Advertising, news- and pressrooms, and packaging-center tour by appt. Free. W. Monique, a third-grader from Santa Catalina school, enthused, "Thank you for giving us a tour of *The Herald* today. It was wonderful and I learned a lot. I learned that you use 8 rolls of newsprint a day and 12 rolls on Sunday. I saw the huge cameras with 200 feet of film. The pictures are made out of dots. To develop the pictures for the newspaper, you have a dark room with a revolving door. I learned that color pictures are made up of only four colors. Thanks."

NAPA, SONOMA, AND LAKE COUNTIES

The Napa-Sonoma area is best known for the vineyards that grow on rolling hills and in the Valley of the Moon. But the country itself is welcoming and best seen from the hot air balloons, gliders, planes, and parachutes now available for the brave of heart. Wineries can be fun for youngsters to visit, not only because the wine-making process is fascinating but because the wine industry is part of California's history and culture. In most wineries, your tour will follow the direction the grape takes, from vineyard delivery to the crushing and the aging vat, and on to the bottles in the tasting rooms. The listed wineries offer the most interesting plants and tours, all of which are free (including the "tasting," which may include grape juice or nonalcoholic wine). We do suggest that you stop at the Oakville Grocery for a loaf of bread and a wedge of cheese to nibble on between tastes.

❯❯ Yountville–Vintage 1870

Highway 29, 6529 Washington Street (P.O. Box 2500), Yountville 94599. (707) 944-2451. Daily, 10–5:30. W.

This lovely historic winery complex is part of the original land grant made to Salvador Vallejo in 1838 and was bought in 1870 for $250 in U.S. gold coin. The brick exterior of the building hasn't changed much, but the interior is now a charming complex of 40 stores including a bakery, toy cellar, and candy store. Restaurants, garden cafes, and picnic areas surround the property.

❯❯ Robert Mondavi Winery

Highway 29, P.O. Box 106, Oakville 94562. (707) 963-9611. Daily, 9–5. Free. W.

Beautifully designed and landscaped by Cliff May, who designed the *Sunset Magazine* building and gardens, the Mondavi Winery offers tours and also jazz concerts and special events, on summer Sundays in the center lawn.

❖ The Silverado Museum

1490 Library Lane, St. Helena 94572. One block east of Main Street (Highway 29). (707) 963-3757. Daily except Mon. and holidays, 12–4. Groups by appt. Free. W.

Robert Louis Stevenson has been associated with the Napa Valley ever since he honeymooned in an abandoned bunkhouse of the Silverado Mine on Mount St. Helena. Today, anyone who grew up on *A Child's Garden of Verses* or *Treasure Island* will appreciate this tribute to the man who wrote them. Portraits of Stevenson abound, including one showing him as a four-year-old with long flowing curls. Original manuscripts, illustrations, the author's toy lead soldiers, tea set, doll, chess set, desk with carved faces, and memorabilia from his plantation in Samoa, plus Henry James's gloves, are neatly displayed in this cheerful museum.

❖ Bale Grist Mill State Historic Park

3369 St. Helena Highway North (Highway 29), 3 miles north of St. Helena. Mail: c/o Napa Valley State Park, 3801 St. Helena Highway North, Calistoga 94515. (707) 963-2236. Demonstrations at 1 and 4 on weekends.

This restored water-powered grist mill was built in 1846 and has been grinding flour ever since. The 36-foot waterwheel is equipped with French buhrs, granite stones used to grind the finest flour. Baking demonstrations (tastings too!) round out the experience. Exhibits provide an orientation to the area as well descriptions of its natural history.

❖ Freemark Abbey

3020 St. Helena Highway North (Highway 29), St. Helena 94574. North of St. Helena. (707) 963-7211. Winery tours daily at 2. Shops open 10–5:30 daily.

The old Freemark Abbey Winery also houses the Hurd Beeswax Candle Factory, along with a restaurant and a gift shop. Weekday visitors may see candles being made by hand, 8:30 to 5, seasonally. And all youngsters will be intrigued by the wooden shutter on the far wall of the inside showroom. It opens to reveal a glass-backed beehive full of bees filling their honeycomb.

❖ Sterling Vineyards

1111 Dunaweal Lane (off Highway 29), Calistoga 94515. (707) 942-3300. Daily except holidays, 10–4:30. Visitor fee, $5; under 16, free.

An aerial tram ride takes visitors high into the hills to see elevated viewing galleries, lulled by the sound of antique English bells ringing the quarter hour and water falling from sculpted fountains.

❧ Sharpsteen Museum & Sam Brannan Cottage

1311 Washington Street, Calistoga 94514. Take Highway 29 to Calistoga; right on Lincoln to Washington. (707) 942-5911. Daily except holidays, 12–4; 10–4 in summer; and by appt. Donation. W.

This museum, given to the city of Calistoga by Ben Sharpsteen, a Disney Studios artist, is dedicated to the preservation and presentation of the history of Calistoga. Calistoga's pioneer history comes alive in the scale model dioramas and shadow boxes. The diorama-mural "Saratoga of the West" covers one wall. Other dioramas depict Robert Louis Stevenson, the railroad depot, the Chinese settlement, and more. Sam Brannan, the founder of Calistoga and the first California millionaire, is present in spirit. One of his cottages has been moved to the site, restored, and furnished authentically, a delight for children and adults.

❧ Old Faithful Geyser of California

1299 Tubbs Lane, Calistoga 94515. North of Calistoga 2 miles. (707) 942-6463. Daily, 9–6 in summer, until 5 in winter. Adults, $3.50; ages 6–12, $2. Group rates. Gift shop and snack bar. Picnic tables available.

One of the more surprising results of the 1989 earthquake is that it made Old Faithful "old erratic." Once one of the few faithful geysers in the world, erupting every 40 minutes almost like clockwork, Old Faithful now shoots forth its plume of boiling water and steam, sometimes 60 feet high, every hour or so, with lapses up to 20 or 30 minutes. But the effect is the same. As one little girl exclaimed, when she viewed the geyser after dark: "Look, Mommy, the geyser is washing the stars."

❧ Petrified Forest

4100 Petrified Forest Road, Calistoga 94515. (707) 942-6667. Daily, 10–5; until 6 in summer. Adults, $3; ages 4–11, $1.

Volcanic eruptions of Mount St. Helena six million years ago formed this forest of petrified redwoods, "discovered" in 1870 and written about by Robert Louis Stevenson. A lovely forest trail passes a 300-foot-long "Monarch" tunnel tree and "the Queen," which was already 3,000 years old when it was buried. On the way out, you'll walk through a specimen shop of fossils and petrified worms, snails, clams, nuts, and wood.

❧ Air Play

The rolling hills and soft wind currents of the area have made the skies here especially accessible. For those who are adventurous, and can afford it, try the following—and check the local Yellow Pages for others. Since companies open and fade with the wind, call for schedules and prices.

Calistoga Gliders. *1546 Lincoln Avenue, Calistoga 94515. (707) 942-5592. Glider rides, instruction, and rental.*
Once in a Lifetime, Inc. *Champagne balloon rides. P.O. Box 795, Calistoga 94515. (800) 722-6665, (707) 942-6541. Three separate balloon companies in Napa Valley and Sonoma County.*
Balloon Aviation of Napa Valley. *2299 Third Avenue, Napa 94558. (707) 252-7067.*
Balloons above the Valley. *5091 St. Helena Highway, P.O. Box 3838, Napa 94559. (800) 464-6824, (800) GO-HOT-AIR, (707) 253-2222.*
Adventures Aloft. *P.O. Box 2500, Yountville 94599. (707) 944-4408. Flights take off from Vintage 1870 after a 6 A.M. breakfast reception.*
Napa Valley Balloons, Inc. *P.O. Box 2860, Yountville 94599. (800) 253-2224, (707) 253-2224.*

❧ Whale watching: *New Sea Angler* and *Jaws*

P.O. Box 1148, Bodega Bay 94923. (707) 875-34995.

Those seeking more down-to-the-sea pleasures may choose to whale watch on the ocean. *New Sea Angler* and *Jaws* head out twice a day on weekends and holidays, December 28 through April, from Bodega Bay. Both vessels also provide year-round, daily salmon and rock cod fishing trips. Special cruises are also offered, on request.

❧ Petaluma Adobe

3325 Adobe Road, Petaluma 94954. East of Highway 101. (707) 726-4871. Daily, 10–5. Tickets are usable at all state parks that day: adults, $2; children, $1. Picnic areas. On summer weekends, kids can help bake bread in the beehive ovens or take part in the dipping of candles. Tours, groups, and Living History Programs.

General Mariano G. Vallejo's ranch house, Rancho Petaluma, was built in 1836 as the centerpiece of a Mexican land grant of 66,000 acres. Here we learned that in Spanish, adobe means *to mix,* and that the thick, naturally insulating bricks were made from clay mixed with water and straw and then dried in the sun. A self-guided tour takes you into the kitchen, workshop, candle room, weaving room, servants' quarters, and the Vallejos' living quarters upstairs—graciously furnished with authentic pieces. Outside, there are huge iron cauldrons, clay ovens, a covered wagon, and the racks on which cowhides, the currency of the period, were stretched out to dry. Farm animals add authentic background sounds. At one time, General Vallejo had one thousand workers on the ranch, and it's not hard, standing on the second-floor porch of Rancho Petaluma, to imagine the bustle of yesteryear.

❖ Petaluma Historical Library–Museum

20 Fourth Street, Petaluma 94952. (707) 778-4398. Thurs.–Mon., 1–4. Free. W.

Downtown in "The Egg Basket of the World," the Petaluma Historical Library–Museum shows rotating and permanent displays, such as one on the local poultry industry and another on local river history. The bust of Chief Solano, photos of General Vallejo, and the Knickerbocker No. 5 fire engine are popular. A third-grader from the Meadow School wrote, "I like the stained glass window, the kitchen and where they did the laundry because it was really fun."

❖ California Coop Creamery

711 Western Street (at Baker), Petaluma 94952. (707) 778-1234. Mon.– Sat., tours on the hour, 11–3. Groups by appt. Free.

The retail outlet of a creamery run cooperatively since 1913 offers daily 30-minute tours and a slide show to display how cheese and butter are made. Free samples.

❖ Marin French Cheese Company

7500 Red Hill Road, Petaluma 94952. Petaluma–Point Reyes Road, 1/4 mile south of Novato Boulevard. (707) 762-6001. Daily, 9–5. Student programs. Free. W.

Situated next to a pond in the rolling, cow-speckled hills between Novato and the coast, this is a perfect destination for an afternoon outing or picnic. A 15-minute tour begins with the 4,000-gallon tank of milk and takes you through the different stages of cheese making—heating the milk, adding the three "cheese" ingredients (culture, enzymes, and starter), and aging. You pass shiny steel tubes and tanks and different aging rooms, each with its own smell. Picnic tables are available, where you can sit and eat a picnic lunch bought on the spot. Kids like the cheese but they love the duck pond.

❖ Sonoma County Farm Trails

Drive from a mushroom farm and eggery in Petaluma to apple farms in Sebastopol, turkey growers, or Christmas tree farms. The map lists Farm Trails members and has a handy product-reference guide. For a copy of the Farm Trails map, send a stamped, self-addressed envelope to: P.O. Box 6032, Santa Rosa 95406.

Local favorites are **California Carnivores** (7020 Trenton-Healdsburg Road, Forestville 95436; 707 838-1630; daily, 10–4, by appt. only in winter) which specializes in insect-eating plants and has 350 varieties on

display. **Krout's Pheasant Farm** (3234 Skillman Lane, Petaluma 94952;
707 762-8613; tours by appt. only) raises exotic fowl, though none are for
sale. At **Pet-a-Llama Ranch** (5505 Lone Pine Road, Sebastopol 94572;
707 823-9394) you can pet llamas large and small, see spinning and
weaving demonstrations, and buy llama products in the shop.

⇾ Sonoma State Historical Park

*20 East Spain Street, Sonoma 95476. (707) 938-1519. Daily, 10–5.
Tickets usable at all state parks that day. Adults, $2; children, $1. W.*

Lachryma Montis, off Third Street West, which was named after its
clear spring, "Tear of the Mountain," was General Vallejo's city house.
Furnished precisely as it was when he lived there with his family, right
down to the photograph of Abraham Lincoln in the hall, the house feels as
if Vallejo just stepped out for a moment. One daughter's painting is on a
wall, along with family photos. Behind the house is the kitchen building
and the Chinese cook's quarters. The Chalet in front was once the storehouse and is now a Vallejo museum containing his books, pictures,
saddles, coach, and cattle brand, various rembrances of his family, and
biographies of 10 of his 16 children.

On the plaza in town you'll walk by Vallejo's first home in Sonoma.
Since a fire in 1867, only the Indian servants' quarters remain. In the
reconstructed **Soldiers Barracks** (built in 1836), there are exhibits representative of Sonoma history, an audio-visual show, and other activities on
weekends. There's a small Indian exhibit in the ranger's building. Also on
the plaza, **The Toscano Hotel,** built in 1858, is a carefully restored mining hotel with cards and whiskey glasses still on the tables waiting for the
card players to return. (Docents give tours on weekends.)

At the far corner of the plaza is **The Mission San Francisco Solano**,
the northernmost and last of the 21 Franciscan missions in California and
the only one established under Mexican, rather than Spanish, rule, in
1823. The padres' quarters is the oldest structure in Sonoma. Visitors can
walk through the building, looking at interesting exhibits, a restored
chapel, watercolors of the missions, furnished rooms of the padres, spurs
and leggings of the *vacqueros*, and other interesting artifacts of mission
life, including the primitively painted chapel. A *ramada* has been constructed in the garden for blacksmith, weaving, bread-baking, and other
period crafts demonstrations. Children can help bake bread on weekends.

During your wanderings you may want to stop in at the **Sonoma
Cheese Factory** (on the plaza at 2 Spain Street, 95476; 707 938-5225;
daily, 9–6), to see a slide show and see young men pounding cheese bags
into Sonoma Jack, and to pick up a picnic, which you can enjoy in the
park across the street.

❯❯ Buena Vista Winery

Old Winery Road, Sonoma 95476. Off East Napa Road, 1 mile from Sonoma. (707) 938-1266. Tasting daily, 10–5. Free.

Buena Vista was the first premium winery in California. Founded in 1857 by the Hungarian count Agoston Haraszthy, who first imported European grape varieties for commercial use, Buena Vista winery is now a California historical landmark. The self-guided tour in hand-dug limestone caves is wonderfully atmospheric. There's a gallery of historic pictures, and there are picnic tables on the grounds.

❯❯ Traintown

20264 Broadway, Sonoma 95476. On the main road into town from San Francisco. (707) 938-3912. Daily in summer and on winter weekends, 10:30–5:30. Adults, $2.60; children, $1.90. W.

A 20-minute trip on the Sonoma Steam Railroad, a quarter-size reproduction of a mountain division steam railroad of the 1890s, takes you over trestles, past trees, lakes, tunnels, and bridges, and into Traintown. While the train takes on water in Lakeview, you can look through the quarter-size miniature mining town and listen to its recorded history. The ducks are normal size, but you still feel like Gulliver in the land of Lilliputians.

❯❯ Jack London State Historic Park

2400 London Ranch Road, Glen Ellen 95442. (707) 938-5216. Museum open daily, 10–5. Grounds, 8–sunset. For the museum and the enlarged park, $5 per car.

"I liked those hills up there above the ranch house. They were beautiful, as you see, and I wanted beauty. So I extended the boundary up to the top of that ridge and all along it…I bought beauty, and I was content with beauty for a while….Do you realize that I devote 2 hours a day to writing and ten to farming?" So wrote Jack London, 1915.

Charmian London built the House of Happy Walls, the finest tribute to a writer in California, as a memorial to her husband. Furnished with the furniture and art gathered for Wolf House, which burned before the Londons could move into it, this museum covers the life of the adventurous young novelist. Once a sailor, prospector, and roustabout, London struggled to gain acceptance as a writer—and you can see a collection of his rejection slips. Photos of the *Snark*, in which the Londons sailed the South Pacific, and treasures collected on their voyages line the walls. The rangers sell London's books "signed" with the stamp London used to save time. A fascinating film taken a few days before his death shows London frolicking with his animals.

London was also an experimental farmer, and the 803 acres of his Beauty Ranch have been purchased by the state. Here you'll see the cottage where he did his writing, concrete silos, the distillery, stallion barn, log bathhouse, and blacksmith's shop. A trail leads to the still-extant Wolf House ruins and to London's grave. Picnic areas.

❧ Union Hotel Restaurant
Main Street (P.O. Box 4257), Occidental 95465. (707) 874-3555. Lunch: Mon.–Sat, 11:30–1:30; $5–$7. Dinners: Mon.–Sat., 2–9, and Sun. and holidays, 11:30–8; $7–$16. Mangia!

Dining at the Union Hotel, which has been in business since 1879, is more than just a meal, it's an experience: Italian food served family style on a plastic red-checked tablecloth with more food than you can possibly eat. One dinner consisted of salami and cheese, bean vinaigrette, salad, lentil soup, zucchini fritters, ravioli, vegetables, your choice of chicken, duck, or steak, good sourdough bread and butter, potatoes, and side dishes. One person in your party could simply order soup and salad, or just the pasta dinner, and you'd still have a bag for tomorrow's lunch. A half-price child's dinner is available. The frequent waits are made bearable by the game room or a walk through the main street of the town.

❧ Redwood Empire Ice Arena
1667 West Steele Lane, Santa Rosa 95403. (707) 546-7147. Sat. and Sun. year-round: 12:30–2:30 and 3–5. Summer: Mon.–Fri., 2:30–5. Winter: Mon. and Wed., 12:30–2; Tues., Thurs., and Fri., 4–5:30. Adults, $6.50; ages 12–17, $5.50; under 12, $4; plus $1 skate rental. Christmas show: (707) 546-3385. Snoopy's Gallery and Gift Shop: (707) 546-3385; 10–6 daily.

Snoopy may skate here incognito, but everyone will enjoy skating in this Alpine wonderland, which the creator of "Peanuts" built for his kids. Hours are complicated because there are frequent shows, so call before setting out. And reserve for one of the shows. The gift store boasts the largest collection of Snoopy merchandise in the world, sized from four inches to five feet, as well as a collection of Charlie Schulz's favorite drawings and awards.

❧ Sonoma County Museum
425 Seventh Street (just off Highway 101), Santa Rosa 95401. (707) 579-1500. Wed.–Sun., 11–4. Free.

The Sonoma County Museum, located in a beautifully restored 1910 post office building, preserves and honors the rich heritage of Sonoma

County. Exhibits change and cover a wide spectrum in both time and subject, from the Native American epoch through the Victorian age to today. Cultural vignettes, special exhibits for children, and the Hart Collection of California landscape art also make the museum worth a visit.

The nearby **Codding Museum of Natural History** focuses on local, regional, and worldwide natural history (557 Summerfield Road, Santa Rosa 95405; 707 539-0556; Wed.–Sun., 11–4; free).

➤ The Church of One Tree–Robert L. Ripley Memorial Museum

492 Sonoma Avenue, Santa Rosa 95401. In Julliard Park at Santa Rosa Avenue. (707) 576-5233. Mar.–Oct., Wed.–Sun., 11–4. Adults, $1.50; ages 7–17 and seniors, 75 cents.

Nestled in tall redwoods, this little church, built from *one* tree, houses personal articles and drawings of the Believe-It-Or-Not man. A wax figure of Ripley looks out at photos of himself with Will Rogers and Shirley Temple, and at newspaper clippings, and samplings of the curiosities he collected. You might hear some of the "Believe-It-Or-Not" radio shows or see video clips of his travel films, movies, and TV shows. A motion picture is in the works to celebrate his 100th birthday, December 25, 1993.

➤ Jesse Peter Native American Art Museum

Santa Rosa Junior College, 1501 Mendocino Avenue, Santa Rosa 95401. (707) 527-4479. Mon., Tues., Wed., and Fri., 12–4; Thurs., 11–3 and by appt. Closed holidays and school vacations. Call for events schedule. Free.

Native American arts are found in this bustling tiny center. Southwest pottery, California basketry, Plains beadwork, Northwest Coast art, sculpture, a Klamath River dugout canoe, and grinding stones are part of a continuing exhibit. There are three permanent house models: a Pomo roundhouse, a Klamath River "xonta," and a Southwest pueblo. Tours include hands-on activities such as grinding acorns, playing Indian gambling games, and using pump drills. Native American drum and dance groups and Native American arts and crafts sales and demonstrations are scheduled regularly.

➤ Windsor Waterworks & Slides

8225 Conde Lane, Windsor 95492. Next to Highway 101, 6 miles north of Santa Rosa. (707) 838-7360. Weekends in May; daily, mid-June through Labor Day. All-day tickets, weekdays: $10.95 for adults, $9.95 for those 12 and under. All-day tickets, weekends: $11.95 and $9.95. Slide Ride, $3 per

*half hour. All day, pool and grounds only: $4.95 for adults, $3.95 for ages
12 and under. Group discounts and events, such as birthday parties and
exclusive rental of the park after Labor Day, encouraged. Call for operating
schedule.*

Imagine lying down on a foam rubber mat, taking off down a 42-foot
drop, speeding 400 feet through tunnels, around spirals, and up and over
slips—and finally landing in a pool. This adventure in family parks offers
four separate waterslides, picnic grounds, a large swimming pool, Ping-
Pong tables, volleyball court, horseshoe pits, a wading pool, video arcade,
playground, and splash fountain.

❧ Healdsburg Museum
*221 Matheson Street, Healdsburg 95448. (707) 431-3325. Tues.–Sat.,
12–5. Free.*

Fine examples of Pomo Indian basketry and crafts, antique firearms,
and 19th-century costumes and tools combine with collections of the
town newspapers dating back to 1878 and over 5,000 original historic
photographs to make this a worthwhile visit.

❧ Canoe Trips on the Russian River
*W. C. "Bob" Trowbridge, 20 Healdsburg Avenue, Healdsburg 95448. (800)
640-1386. Each canoe, $32. Over 6 years of age only. Reservations suggested.
Call or write for information.*

The picturesque, winding Russian River is perfect for family canoe
trips. It's safe and lovely but can also be fast enough to be exciting. One-
and two-hour and also half-day trips are available and there's chicken
barbecue on weekends in summer. Swimmers only!

❧ Cloverdale Historical Society Museum
*215 North Cloverdale Boulevard, Cloverdale 95425. (707) 894-2067.
Mon.–Fri., 9–3 and by appt. Donation.*

A charming collection of Victoriana snuggles in this 1870 Victorian
red, white, blue, and brick house lacy with gingerbread and a picket
fence. The butter churns and tins in the general store and the doll collection in the bedroom look right at home.

❧ Fort Ross State Historic Park
*Highway 1, 12 curving miles north of Jenner. Mailing address: 30 East
Spain Street, Sonoma 95476. (707) 847-3246. Daily, 10–4:30. Cars, $5;
$4 for a senior's car.*

California history seems especially romantic in this scenic spot. The Russian Chapel, with a bell you can ring in front, is as spare and quiet as it was when the fort was sold to John Sutter in 1841. Visitors can climb up into the eight-sided blockade tower and seven-sided blockhouse to look out over the little beach and inlet where Russian fur merchants used to trade with the Indians. The Visitors Center contains displays and artifacts from the Native American, Russian, and ranch eras. Don't forget to toss a penny into the wishing well!

✥ Lake County Museum

Old Courthouse, 255 North Main Street, Lakeport. Mail: 255 North Forbes Street, 95451. (707) 263-4555. Oct.–Apr., Wed.–Sat., 10–4. May–Sept., Sun., 11–4. Donation.

Beautifully woven Pomo baskets and hunting traps are nicely displayed in this country museum, along with arrowheads, spears, and small tools. Firearms used to tame the West, such as the Kentucky Long and the Slotterbeck made in Lakeport in the late 1800s, are also intriguing. Other displays include turn-of-the-century clothing and household items and samples of the semiprecious gems and minerals found in Lake County. Did you know that the "Lake County diamond," a natural or faceted quartz crystal, could be pink or lavender? The museum is also the home of the Lake County Genealogical Society, which boasts hundreds of books to help you find your roots.

✥ Anderson Marsh State Historic Park

P.O. Box 672, Lower Lake 95457. Take Route 20 to 53 or 29 to Lower Lake, then continue straight on 53. (707) 994-0688/279-2267. Farmhouse: Fri.–Sun., 10–4; 8–5 in summer. Parking fee, $2. Park: Wed.–Sun., 10–5. Cultural History Days and Living History Programs. Groups by appt.

Costumed docents wander through the old, two-story Anderson ranch house, lost in their roles in yesteryear. Outdoors, archaeologists working on the ancient Pomo Indian encampments nearby talk about life centuries ago. Ranchers offer visitors many hands-on and "work" experiences. The community has worked together to restore the 1855 Anderson farmhouse with authentic antiques augmenting the original cozy furnishings. On an oak-covered ridge above the marsh, a sweeping expanse of grassy lowland, the Cultural Heritage Council is working with local Pomo to reconstruct a Pomo village. Students from 12 to 70 camp out and attend the field school, where the homework can be heavy digging.

REDWOOD COUNTRY:
MENDOCINO, HUMBOLDT, AND DEL NORTE COUNTIES

Redwood country is one of the most beautiful areas in America. Stately redwoods line the roads "as far as the fog flows," and the Pacific Ocean crashes into the shoreline. Some of the beaches are craggy and surrounded by dangerous currents. Others are calm and protected, with long empty stretches just made for solitary walks.

You can dash up from San Francisco on Highway 101 or you can spend hours winding along the coastline on Highway 1. You can enjoy the Victoriana of Ferndale and Eureka or you can lose yourself in the tiny fishing villages of Rockport and Noyo. Whale watching is a popular pastime from December to April. The waters may be too cold to swim in, but the fish thrive and are there for the catching.

You can get away from it all in the sylvan glens along the Avenue of the Giants, marveling at your smallness next to a 300-foot tree. To show the aims, methods, and benefits of industrial forest management within the redwood region, several firms have made demonstration forests available to the public. Tours are self-guided and there are restrooms and picnic areas available. You'll learn that only one percent of the tree is living—only the tips of its roots, the leaves, buds, flowers, seed, and a single thin layer of cells sheathing the tree. You'll see Douglas firs, white firs, and redwood residuals—the redwood trees that have sprung up from seeds and sprouts. You'll find the forests along Highway 128, on new and old Highways 101, and on Highway 299.

Redwood country lets you set your own pace—there are many places to see and things to do close to each other, and there are enough parks and beaches for you to relax or picnic in, whenever the mood strikes. It's a great getaway for a weekend or a week.

❖ Point Arena Lighthouse & Museum
P.O. Box 11, Point Arena 95468. (707) 882-2777. Daily, 11–2:30; summer weekends and holidays, 10–3:30. Closed Thanksgiving and Christmas days only. Adults, $2; children, 50 cents.

If you've ever dreamed about living in history, this is a good way to do it. The lighthouse keepers have restored the lighthouse, museum, and three of the large homes on the lighthouse station to rent to vacationers. Rental fees and fees from whale watching and guided tours help maintain the site. The first Point Arena lighthouse had to be destroyed after the 1906 earthquake; a new 115-foot tower with a Fresnel lens began flashing its guiding beacon in 1908. An automatic rotating beacon was installed in

1977. The museum is housed in the 1869 Fog Signal Building, next to the lighthouse.

❖ Mendocino Headlands State Park and Ford House Visitors Center

Main Street (P.O. Box 1387), Mendocino 95460. (707) 937-5397/937-5804. Mon.–Sat., 10:30–4:30; Sun., 12–4. Videos and headlands walks. Groups by appt.

The Ford House, the second house to be built in the town of Mendocino, was a wedding gift from J. B. Ford to his bride, Martha Hayes Ford of Connecticut, in 1854. Today, it is the Visitors Center, interpreting the natural environment of the area and telling of the history of Mendocino and the surrounding areas. It is also a gallery exhibiting work by local artists. The star of the place is a recently constructed four-by-eight-foot scale model of Mendocino village as it was on December 14, 1890, with its 358 buildings including sheds, outhouses, and 34 water towers, built on a scale of 3/64 inches to the foot. Buildings were carved by artist Len Peterson of balsa wood and secured to a foam-core terrain that replicates the surface contours of the village. There are tramway tracks for the lumber vehicles, a 3 1/8-inch-tall Presbyterian Church, eight hotels, four boardinghouses, a bank, two dressmakers, and a cobbler's store.

Once an old lumber port, Mendocino is now a mecca for driftwood collectors, artists, and tourists. The town has appeared in many movies and has interesting little streets to browse along when it gets too foggy for beachcombing. Among the highlights are the **Mendocino Art Center** (54200 Little Lake Street, 95460; 707 937-5819), which is open 10 to 5 daily and has special movies and shows at night; **The Mendocino Ice Cream Company** (on Main; 937-5884), and the **Village Toy Store**, the kite and frisbee store (on Lansing; 937-4633).

The old **Masonic Lodge Hall**, at Lansing and Ukiah, with its massive redwood sculpture of Father Time and the Maiden, carved from one piece of redwood, is a landmark.

The Kelley House Historical Museum (45007 Albion Street, or Box 922, 95460; 707 937-5791; daily, 1–4; donation) is a pleasant step back in time. The nearby **Temple of Kwan Ti**, one of the first buildings in Mendocino, may be seen by appointment.

❖ Mendocino Coast Botanical Gardens

18220 North Highway 1 (6 miles north of Mendocino), Fort Bragg 95437. (707) 964-4352. Mar.–Oct., daily, 9–5; Nov.–Feb., 9–4. Retail nursery *and gift shop. Adults, $5; seniors, $4; student groups and those under 12, free. Group discounts and tours. W.*

Forty-seven acres of formal gardens, coastal pine forest, fern canyons, and ocean bluff explode with multicolored flowers and teem with protected wildlife, including 60 species of birds. Rhododendrons bloom in April and May; perennials, from May to October. The heath blooms all winter, when you can see gray whale migration. Picnickers are welcome. One youngster wrote, "That was the most fun place I have ever been. I liked all the flowers that were there. I liked all the trails; I liked all the places, especially the ocean. I liked when we got to eat and played games. We did work and we almost got lost too in The Botanical Gardens."

❖ Guest House Museum

Main Street (c/o City Hall, 416 North Franklin), Fort Bragg, 95437. (707) 961-2840. Wed.–Sun., 10–4. Donation.

This gift to the city from the Georgia Pacific Company houses historical pictures of the logging industry, a huge bellows, mementos of the loggers, and models of ships. Films and talks contrast the difference between logging's industrial present and its rugged past. Be sure to walk down to the foot of Redwood Avenue to see the huge slice of redwood that was 1,753 years old in 1843.

Nearby, at the foot of Walnut Street, is the **Georgia Pacific Nursery** (9–4 weekdays, Apr.–Nov.), which holds four million trees. A display room explains reforestation and timber management. An arboretum, nature trails, and picnic tables are available. A free packet of redwood seeds is mailed to each visiting family.

❖ The Skunk Railroad

Skunk Depot, Main and Laurel, Fort Bragg. (707) 964-6371. Reserve by writing to California Western Railroad, P.O. Box 907, Fort Bragg 95437. Half and full-day trips from and to Fort Bragg and Willits to Northspur are available at prices ranging from about $9 for children for a three-hour trip to $23 for adults for the full day.

The Skunk Railroad, named for the smell the first gas engines used to cast over the countryside, has been making passenger trips from Fort Bragg to Willits since 1911. During the 40-mile trip the train crosses 30 trestles and bridges, goes through two tunnels, twists and turns over spectacularly curved track, and travels from the quiet Noyo riverbed to high mountain passes through redwood forest. The bouncy diesel Skunk is well worth the price and time. If it's summer, try the open observation car.

There's also a train from Willits to Eureka. **The Redwood Coast Railway Company** (299 East Commercial Street; 800 482-7100) runs along the Earl River through redwood forest to Old Town, 145 miles away. Call for times and prices.

➣ Mendocino County Museum

400 East Commercial Street, Willits 95490. (707) 459-2736. Wed.–Sat., 10–4:30. Free. W.

The Mendocino County Museum is a storehouse of memories, dreams, and hard-won lessons of survival amid the rugged beauty of California's North Coast. Exhibits use local artifacts to celebrate and explain the life and times of Mendocino County. Oral history interviews capture living memories on tape. Collections of Pomo and Yuki baskets represent the vanished ancestors and today's descendants of the region's Native Americans. The danger and excitement of everyday work in the redwoods is recalled through living history programs featuring restored logging artifacts discovered in the Mendocino woods. Changing exhibits provide fresh experiences for museum visitors.

➣ The Drive-Thru Tree

Old Highway 101 (P.O. Box 10), Leggett 95585. (707) 925-6363. Daily, 9–5; in summer, 8 until dark. Each car $3.

This large, chandelier-shaped, 315-foot redwood was tunneled in 1934, and a standard-size contemporary car just fits through. It's 21 feet in diameter and, in spite of the tunnel, is still alive. The winding dirt road leading to the tree takes you right to a gift shop and to the highway. There are 200 acres of nature trails and picnic areas by the side of a lake that is home to geese. There are also logging relics on the grounds. Kids like the log with a hole you can crawl into.

➣ Confusion Hill and Mountain Train Ride

75001 North Highway 101 (15 miles south of Garberville), Piercy 95467. (707) 925-6456. Daily, 9–6. Confusion Hill: adults, $2.50; ages 6–12, $1.25. Mountain Train Ride: Apr.–Sept., adults, $2.50; ages 3–12, $1.25.

The miniature Mountain Train follows many switchbacks to take you one and one-quarter miles up to the summit of a redwood mountain, through a tunnel tree, and back down. Try the other experience at Confusion Hill, a spot where gravity is defied. Facing front, you seem to be standing sideways; water runs uphill; your friends shrink or grow taller in front of you. Is seeing really believing?

◈ Avenue of the Giants

Humboldt Redwoods State Park, P.O. Box 100, Weott 95571. (707) 946-2311. Day use, $4; camping, $14 per night. Reduced senior and winter rates. Visitors Center, next to Burlington Campground, 2 miles south of Weott. (707) 946-2263. Daily, 9–5.

Standing tall as a nominee for the most spectacular 33 miles anywhere is this bypass road winding leisurely beneath 300-foot trees. One of the few species to have survived from the time of the dinosaurs, the redwoods are majestic, awesome trees to behold. You'll drive through a protected wilderness of soaring trees and moss- and fern-carpeted landscape occasionally spotted with deer. Founder's Grove, Rockefeller Forest, and Childen's Forest are some of the best of the special groves. The Chimney Tree near Phillipsville, the Immortal Tree near Redcrest, and the Drive-Thru Tree in Myers Flat are more commercial stopping places. The Visitors Center displays the flora and fauna and history of the area and has an interesting slide show on request.

◈ Pacific Lumber Company

P.O. Box 37, Scotia 95565. South of Eureka 27 miles. (707) 764-2222. Mill tours, Mon.–Fri., 7:30–10:30 and 12–2:30. Mill closed for July Fourth and Christmas weeks. Museum open in summer, 8–4. Free. Demonstration Forest open to the public in summer, 4 1/2 miles south of Scotia. Free.

Scotia is one of the last company-owned towns in the country. The Pacific Lumber Company was established in 1869, and the present town of Scotia, originally known as Forestville, was established in 1910. During the summer, obtain a pass for the mill tour at the Scotia museum. Logging equipment is on display outside, and inside there are historic photographs. You can watch a video about the lumber company. On the mill tour, you'll see how trees become lumber products. The first step is the most impressive: a debarker that uses high water pressure to peel the bark off the log. Signs posted along the catwalk explain the various functions of the mill. Some sections are noiser than others.

According to Carmen, "It was loud inside and the best part about the mill was when the debarker blasted the bark off the trees. I also liked it when the one man sharpened the saws, that must have been hard work."

Don't miss the Scotia fish-rearing pond, built by Pacific Lumber to enhance the fisheries in the nearby Eel River. Visitors pass by the pond right after leaving the parking lot, before entering the mill.

◈ Depot Museum

4 Park Street, Fortuna 95540. (707) 725-2495. Daily, 12–5 in summer. Closed Thur. and Fri., Sept.–May. Donation. W.

The 1893 train depot is now a small museum housing Fortuna memories of the loggers, farmers, Indians, and the railroad. The old teletyper is at the ready; fancy dresses and shoes wait for the next dance; fishing poles and tackle stand waiting for the next fishing trip; and pictures and school books round out the collection. The three old marriage certificates are lovely. The museum is located in Rohner Park, a lovely family park with picnic tables and playground equipment. The Depot offers a handicap map of nearby attractions free, for disabled friends.

Visitors in autumn may want to stop by **Clendenen's Cider Works** (Twelfth Street and Newburg Road; 707 725-2123) to see the mill in action and buy fresh cider.

❖ Ferndale Museum

Shaw and Third streets (Box 431), Ferndale 95536. (707) 786-4466. Feb.– May and Oct.–Dec.: Wed.–Sat., 11–4; Sun., 1–4. June–Sept.: Tues.–Sat., 11– 4; Sun., 1–4. Closed Jan. Adults, $1; 16 and under, 50 cents; 6 and under free, when accompanying an adult. Group demonstrations and lectures by appt.

A blacksmith shop with a working forge, antique farming and logging equipment, and a working seismograph are permanent exhibits, along with rotating collections that show the lifestyles, work habits, and activities of Ferndale's ancestors. Since most of the successful businessmen made their money with farms, their Victorian homes were called "Butterfat Palaces" and the town was called "Cream City." Ferndale, a restored and repainted Victorian town, is a wonderful place to spend time.

❖ Fort Humboldt State Historic Park

3431 Fort Avenue (off Highway 101), Eureka 95501. (707) 445-6567. Daily, 9–5. Free.

High on a windy hill, Fort Humboldt is primarily an outdoor museum of the logging industry. Old machinery is accompanied by large display boards telling what it was like to be a logger in the 19th century. A logger's cabin is furnished with a stove, a bed, a shelf of cans of beans, and a "pin-up" calendar. You learn how to "fall" a tree (the falling branches are called widow makers) and then see how it is dragged out of the forest and cut up. One logger notes that it's "a shame to wash clothes while they can still bend." An 1884 Falk locomotive and an 1892 Andersonia locomotive are on view. Old Fort Humboldt, where U. S. Grant served as a staff officer in the 1850s, is nearby. Fort Humboldt was retired as a military post in August 1870. The land and the one remaining building, the hospital, completed in 1863, were sold to W. S. Cooper in 1893 for $6,500. Today the hospital has been restored and is used as a museum.

A short drive away are the only two covered bridges in the area. Take Highway 101 south to Elk River Road and follow it along to either Zane or Berta road. The bridges are covered not to protect them from snow but to protect the lumber from rain—boarding them up preserves the wood longer and is less expensive than constant repainting.

❖ Clarke Memorial Museum

240 E Street (at Third), Eureka 95501. (707) 443-1947. Tues.–Sat., 12–4. Free. W.

This large regional history museum is housed in a palatial 1912 bank. A recent addition is devoted to the Native American Indian culture of northwestern California. The world's largest and most complete collections of Hoopa, Yurok, and Karuk regalia and basketry is at the Clarke, with over 1,200 artifacts displayed. There are also extensive collections on the development of Humboldt County: shipbuilding, logging, milling, firearms, furniture, textiles, and Victorian decorative arts.

Alyssa and Courtney of Scotia noted, "We had a blast looking at all the things in the museum. Some of the baskets were really rad. We loved the children's corner. We especially liked the 3-D thing. It was cool. Altogether it was fun."

The Clarke Museum is located in Eureka's Old Town, the original, restored, commercial district on the shore of Humboldt Bay. This district of Victorian commercial and residential buildings, crowned by the remarkable Carson Mansion (on Second and M streets, not open to the public), the greatest Victorian in California, includes many bookstores and boutiques. Be sure to visit the crafts shop of the Northern California Indian Development Council on F Street, next to the Bon Bonière Ice Cream Parlor. There's a self-guided tour if you want to see how oysters are processed on the shoreline (call 707 442-2947).

❖ Humboldt Bay Maritime Museum

1410 Second Street, Eureka 95501. (707) 444-9440. Daily, 11–4. Donation. W.

Nautical displays are housed in a replica of the McFarlan House, built in 1852, the oldest home in Eureka. A Fresnel lighthouse lens, a hand-operated bilge pump, a salmon gear pulley, old navigation instruments, a fathometer, an early radar unit, cork and glass floats, and a porthole from the cruiser USS *Milwaukee*, which was wrecked on the Samoa peninsula in 1917, are shown. There have been hundreds of wrecks off the entrance to Humboldt Bay, and the museum's dedicated volunteers continuously dive for and salvage remains of these relics for display.

⇛ The Humboldt Bay Harbor Cruise, M/V Madaket Bay Tour

Foot of C Street, Eureka 95501. Call (707) 442-1910 for times and prices.

The 75-minute cruise aboard this venerable vessel, a 1910 ferry, takes in the oyster beds, pelican roosts, saw mills, egret rookery, and a former Indian village, and includes history of the area.

⇛ Sequoia Park Zoo

3414 W Street (at Glatt), Eureka 95501. (707) 442-6552. Tues.–Sun., 10–5; until 7 in summer. Children's Petting Zoo (only in June): Tues.–Sun., 11:30–3:30. Free. W.

Located in the heart of the redwoods, the Sequoia Park Zoo houses an excellent variety of both local and exotic animals including the gibbon, otter, emu, prairie dog, reticulated python, black bear, and Pacific giant salamander. The zoo is part of Sequoia Park, which encompasses picnic areas, a playground, flower gardens, a duck pond, and 54 acres of North Coast redwoods.

⇛ Samoa Cookhouse

Samoa Road (445 West Washington), Eureka 95501. (707) 442-1659. Breakfast: $2.95, $4.40, and $5.85. Lunch: $3.35, $4.45, and $5.95. Dinner: ages 3–6, $4.45; 7–11, $6.95; adults, $10.65.

Delicious, affordable family-style meals are served seven days a week in this old lumber-camp cookhouse that once served as relief quarters for shipwreck victims. The long tables are set as they were in 1885, with red and white checked cloths and large bottles of catsup. Our breakfast consisted of huge amounts of orange juice, coffee, delicious French toast, and sausage. Dinner the night before included thick cuts of ham and sole with all the fixings, and peach pie. Before or after the meal, wander through the adjoining rooms to see an assemblage of logger's boots, dinner bells, kitchen utensils, and a steam coffeemaker that once served 500 men three times a day.

⇛ Hoopa Tribal Museum

Hoopa Valley Indian Reservation, General Delivery, Hoopa 95546. Highway 96, off Highway 299 West; museum is in Hoopa Shopping Center across Trinity River Bridge. (916) 625-4110. Weekdays, 9–5; also Sat. in summer. Free.

Stone implements, dishes, tools, baskets, and dance regalia of the Hoopa Indians—"the people who live up the river," as named by Jedediah

Smith's Yurok guide—are shown here, along with items from other tribes, such as the Yurok and Karuk, the Dakotas, and Alaskan tribes. Many of the Hoopa items are on loan from local residents, for this is a living museum, run by members of the Hoopa tribe, of artifacts still used regularly in traditional tribal ceremonies in this "Land of the Natinixwe." *Where the Trails Return*, a documentary video explaining the Hoopa culture, tradition, and government, can be viewed at the museum, which will also arrange tours of the reservation.

❖ Humboldt State University Natural History Museum
Corner of 13 and G streets, Arcata 95521. (707) 826-4479. Tues.–Sat., 10–4. Donation. Groups, special programs, speakers, field trips. W.

Displays of various life forms from more than 500 million years ago to present times are presented for a self-guided tour that takes about an hour. Changed periodically, the displays are arranged to emphasize the evolution of life forms and the relationships of living creatures with their environment. The centerpiece of the museum is the amazing Maloney collection of fossils from Africa, Europe, and North and South America.

❖ Humboldt State University Marine Laboratory
P.O. Box 690, Trinidad 95570. Off Highway 101 at Edwards and Ewing. (707) 677-3671. Mon.–Fri., 8–4. Free. W.

Located near Land's End, in the picturesque fishing village of Trinidad, this working laboratory is open to the public for self-guided tours. Hallway aquariums hold rare and common mollusks and crustaceans, and fresh- and saltwater fish. Varicolored anemones, walleye surf perches, Siamese tigerfish, and shovel-nose catfish were there for our visit, along with a tame wolf eel and a small black octopus. Exhibits change regularly. Special school programs.

Stop at the **Trinidad Lighthouse** on your way to the lab. This is the spot where the Spaniards landed on Trinity Sunday in 1775. The original gear system of descending weights still works to turn the light, but the original two-ton bell is for display only.

Patrick's Point State Park, five miles north of the lab along the shore, has natural history displays at park headquarters (707 677-3570; $5 admission for each car; W). Outdoors, there is a Yurok village constructed to look as it might have a century ago.

⤜ Simpson Korbel Forest Nursery

P.O. Box 1169, Arcata 95521. Highway 299 near Blue Lake in Korbel. (707) 822-0371 ext. 539. Free.

Tours by appointment only, to see the care and nurturing of our forests.

⤜ Mad River State Fish Hatchery

1660 Hatchery Road, Blue Lake. Mail: 1660 Hatchery Road, Arcata 95521. (707) 822-0592. Daylight hours. Groups by appt. only. Free. W.

Baby salmon, steelhead, and trout can be seen and fed here. There is fishing (also wheelchair accessible) adjacent to the hatchery. By the way, the river is not ferocious. It was named for a fight between Joe Greek and L. K. Wood, two explorers of the region, in 1849. One Headstarter named Nathan wrote, "It was nice feeding the fish. I liked when the fish jumped. It was nice letting the fish free."

⤜ Prairie Creek Redwoods State Park

Highway 101 North, Orick 95555. North of Orick 6 miles. (707) 488-2171. Day-use fee, $5. Camping, $14 per night, Memorial Day to Labor Day; $12 per night the rest of the year. Junior ranger programs five days a week for children 6–12. Call for times and topics. W.

Roosevelt elk roam this state park and can be seen grazing on the meadow outside the Visitors Center. Inside the center you'll see an interesting exhibit on the elk and the trees, ferns, flowers, and animals in the area. The most extraordinary object is a madrone tree that grew to envelop the skull of an elk. Fine nature trails lead from the center. On one is a redwood hollowed out by fire that is still living. Sixty-five school children have been inside it at one time.

Just south of the park, on Highway 101, is the **Prairie Creek Fish Hatchery** (707 488-2253; 8–5 daily; free), which raises king and silver salmon and coastal cutthroat and rainbow trout.

Just north of Orick, at Bald Hills Junction, the **Arcata Redwood Company's Mill "A"** welcomes visitors to view operations from an overhead catwalk. A Forest Renewal Exhibit is five miles farther north. Four miles south on Highway 101, the **Rellim Demonstration Forest** offers a free self-guiding tour (P.O. Box 247, Crescent City 95531; 707 464-3144).

❖ Trees of Mystery

Redwood Highway/U.S. 101 (P.O. Box 96), Klamath 95548. South of Crescent City 16 miles. (707) 482-5613. Daily, 8–7, except until 9 in summer and 5 in winter. Closed holidays. Adults, $5.50; seniors, $4.50; ages 6–12, $2.75. Group discounts. Trail closes 15 minutes before the rest, depending on daylight. Gift shop. W.

A talking 49-foot-tall Paul Bunyan greets you at the entrance, and then you walk through a hollowed redwood log into a forest of redwoods, where recorded music and explanations take you past trees such as the "Fallen Giant" and the "Elephant Tree," and the immense and moving "Cathedral Tree." Back down the hill is our favorite section—Paul Bunyan's "Trail of Tall Tails"—where you hear how Babe the Blue Ox was found, how the Grand Canyon was dug, and how Sourdough Sam makes his pancakes. (His recipe includes the lard from one summer-fatted bear.) Indians called this "a place of spirits," and the End of the Trail Museum in the gift shop offers an extensive array of clothes and artifacts of tribes ranging from the Mississippi to the Pacific and north to the Aleutians.

The Drive-Through Tree five miles south, on Highway 101 at the north end of the Klamath River Bridge (known for its decorative golden bears), is worth a short visit.

❖ Undersea World

Highway 101 South, Crescent City 95531. South of the Oregon border 20 miles. (707) 464-3522. Daily: summer, 8–8; winter, 9–5. Adults, $5.95; seniors and teens, $4.95; ages 5–12, $2.95. Group rates.

Thousands of marine specimens live in this interactive sea environment. At the touchable tide pool you can pick up a starfish, tickle sea anemones, and touch many types of sea critters. You can look a shark in the eye, see bat rays flying through the water, pet an octopus, and see a sea lion show.

❖ Del Norte Historical Society Museum

577 H Street, Crescent City 95531. (707) 464-3922. Mon.–Fri., 10–4. Adults, $1.50; children under 12, 50 cents.

The 1935 version of *Last of the Mohicans* was filmed in Crescent City, and this museum, once a county jail, has many photos of the Indians who appeared in it. A Yurok bark house and stick games, headdresses, beads, dolls, and baskets of the Tolowa, Pomo, Hoopa, and Yurok tribes are shown, as are photos of Crescent City since its beginnings, with lots of "before and after" shots of the 1964 tidal wave. Unicycles, jail cells, a moonshine still, pioneer clothing, the Fresnel lens from Point St. George lighthouse, and other collections by local residents bring new life to local history.

≫ Battery Point Lighthouse

P.O. Box 396, Crescent City 95531. (707) 464-3089. Apr.–Sept.: Wed.–Sun., 10–4, tide permitting. Adults, $2; under 12, 50 cents.

Battery Point Lighthouse is located offshore from Crescent Ciy on a little island accessible only at low tide. The guided tour covers most of the lighthouse and most of its history. The beacon on display is the fourth one used in this lighthouse. The fifth beacon is in use now, as the lighthouse is active as a private aid to navigation. Visitors can see an old log book, banjo clock, shipwreck photos, and nautical mementos. Although many have hopes of being stranded by the tide, the wealth of native plants and view of the ocean from the tower will make up for their disappointment in finding themselves safely back on the mainland.

≫ Ship Ashore

P.O. Box 75, Smith River 95567. On Highway 101, 3 miles south of the Oregon border. (707) 487-3141. Daily, 10–5:30. Free.

This 160-foot former luxury yacht, which also served the U.S. Navy during World War II, is now a landlocked gift shop with a complete naval and historical museum under the main deck. The wheelhouse is full of ship models—from a 17th-century man o'war to a World War II vessel—and kids can take a turn at the wheel itself. An autograph and the address of Nujuo Fujita, the only Japanese pilot to drop a firebomb on the United States, is on the wall. Downstairs you'll find a potpourri of memories and souvenirs that range from a 1910 country doctor's kit to Alaskan boots, stuffed owls and armadillos, an extensive shell collection, shop blueprints, swords and uniforms, clothes and necklaces from the Edward Lopez family of the Tolowa tribe, and a fascinating pirate's den that presents the lore and rules pirates lived by.

THE BIG VALLEY

✴ SOLANO, SACRAMENTO, AND SAN JOAQUIN COUNTIES

Today, the Sacramento area is the political heartland of the state of California. Two hours away from San Francisco, the city of Sacramento is worth a visit to get a feeling for how the world's eighth largest economy functions.

At different times, the capital of California has been Benicia, Vallejo, and San Jose. The state capitol is now firmly ensconced under the beautifully restored dome in Sacramento. The rich farmland surrounding the city is reflected in the 40-acre Capital Park in the city, and you will appreciate the mix of urban, suburban, and rural settings, which symbolize the variety of California's lifestyles.

Stockton, south of Sacramento, is one entrance to the Gold Country. Visitors will find rolling hills and farmland dotted by small towns. Stockton is named in honor of Commodore Robert Stockton, who led the forces that took over California for the United States in 1847. The lakes and peaceful atmosphere of the San Joaquin Valley add to the ambience of the area, and water-sports lovers will find ample opportunities for houseboating, skiing, fishing, and every kind of boating.

❖ Marine World/Africa USA

Marine World Parkway, Vallejo 94589. Off Highways 80 and 37. (707) 643-ORCA/644-4000. Wed.–Sun. and holidays: in winter, 9:30–5; in summer, daily until 6, until 7 on weekends. Adults, $21.95; over 60, $18.95; ages 4–12, $15.95. Prices cover everything except the elephant and camel rides. Parking, $3. Dolphinstrollers and wheelchairs for rent. Picnic areas. Red & White Ferry from San Francisco's Pier 41: (800) 229-2784. BARTLINK: (707) 648-4666. Season tickets, group discounts available.

Dancing dolphins, killer whales, waterskiing extravaganzas, an ecology theater, and a "gentle jungle" petting area are just some of the many attractions in this remarkable theme park and ecology center. For a real experience, come eye to eye with 15 different species of shark as they swim around you while you move down a crystal-clear tunnel swirling with other fish in coral caves. When the kids tire of looking at the aquarium and other exhibits, they can sit and watch an exciting show or let off steam at the Whale-of-a-Time Playground. There are elephant and camel rides, animal encounters, seals to feed, and dozens of ways to have a wonderful day.

❧ Vallejo Naval & Historical Museum

734 Main Street, Vallejo 94590. (707) 643-0077. Tues.–Sat., 10–4:30. Adults, $1.50; children, 75 cents.

Ship models, murals, and the periscope from the U.S.S. *Baya* attract naval buffs to this small but special museum where revolving exhibits focus on community and naval history.

❧ Herman Goelitz Candy Company

2400 North Watney Way, Fairfield 94533. (707) 428-2838. From Highway 80, take West Texas to Beck Avenue; right to Courage Drive, right on North Watney. Store open Mon.–Fri. Tours by reservation. No open-toed shoes; shoes with soft soles recommended. No children under 6. An informative video begins the 30-minute tour. Free.

"The day I went to the Jelly Belly factory I fell in love. You could see how they make the candy and how they put the chocolate on the raisins. They put the raisins in a barrel and the barrel turned. You'll get samples of candy. You will enjoy it. I did. They have jelly beans in 40 flavors which are very good. The Jelly Belly is an interesting place to go and see how candy is made. You should go. You will have a blast." So gushed Tina Miranda, a fourth-grader at David A. Weir School, Fairfield.

The Goelitz Candy Company has been in business since 1898. Its candy makers invented the jelly bean, after inventing candy corn, in 1926. Gummi products are a recent addition. There are only four calories per jelly bean—and it takes 7 to 10 days to make one.

❧ Vacaville Museum

212 Buck Avenue, Vacaville 95688. (707) 447-4513. Wed.–Sun., 1–4:30. Adults, $1; students, 50 cents. Wed. free. Gift shop. Video theater and special programs. W.

This active museum honors the city's heritage, its founders, and the farmers who settled Solano County. Rotating exhibits such as the Vaca Valley Doll Club's collection and on Victorian dining will interest the whole family.

The **Peña Adobe**, on Highway 80, five miles south of Vacaville, is open during the day for visitors who want to see what rancho life was like.

The Peña Adobe is the original adobe built here, on an ancient Indian site, and some of the Wintu artifacts found during restoration are displayed. There are picnic tables on the grounds.

☣ Lagoon Valley Soaring
5419 Weber Road, Vacaville 95687. (707) 447-4500. Glider rides and sailplane lessons. Daily, 9–5. For one person, $60; two people, $80 and up.

Gliding flights last about 20 to 45 glorious silent minutes, or you can take lessons or just go up for a scenic cruise, in a 1928 Travelaire biplane or, for the more spectacular aerobatic ride, in the Great Lakes–replica biplane.

☣ Suisun Valley Harvest Trails
Farmers and farm stores have put together a map and guide to producers who are open to the public. An afternoon outing to see where our food comes from can be educational as well as entertaining. Youngsters will particularly want to visit the **Suisun Valley Fisheries** (5114 Suisun Valley Road, Suisun Valley; 707 426-1422).

At **The Research Farm** (25344 County Road 95, 1/2 mile north of Road 31, Davis 95616; 916 758-1387; by appointment) you can see an amazing collection of flora and fauna, from llamas and emu to catfish and peacocks to Barbados sheep to sacred lotus plants and comb honey. The Farm also has a special program for bringing animals to the classroom, and offers summer day camps. You may call the same number to arrange for free special interpretive walks in the Quail Ridge Ecological Conservancy on Lake Berryessa in the Vaca Mountains. The conservancy is noted for the native California oak stands and rare bunch grasses, as well as a plethora of protected fauna.

To receive your map, send a stamped, self-addressed envelope to Suisun Valley Harvest Trails (707 421-6790), 200 West Texas Street, Fairfield 94533.

☣ The Nut Tree
Monte Vista Avenue (off Highway 80), Vacaville 95688. (707) 448-6411. Daily, 7 A.M. to 9 P.M. Closed Christmas. Tours by appt.

The Nut Tree is more than a restaurant—it's an enjoyment center. The restaurant is lavishly decorated with rooms facing a huge glass aviary where brilliantly colored birds fly, sing, and eat fruits and seeds. Breakfast, lunch, and dinner prices are moderate, with an emphasis on California fruits and produce. There are theme restaurants and snack bars on the grounds, as well as a huge gift store and a toy store. Rocking horses, a rocking giraffe, play mirrors, and a funny-face play-wall will entice the children. Outside the toy store, they can board a miniature train for a five-minute ride ($1 each, three for $2.50). The family home of the founders of the Nut Tree on the grounds has been restored.

❖ Yolo County Museum

512 Gibson Road, Woodland 95695. Highway 80 to Route 113. (916) 666-1045. Mon. and Tues., 10–4; weekends, 12–4 and by appt. Free.

Housed in the Southern mansion built by William Gibson to remind himself of his Virginia home, this museum records area history as seen through the lives of one family. Each room represents another era and different generation of Gibsons, from 1850 to 1940. The dairy, root cellar, and washroom outside still work. Antique farm equipment, a barn display building, an herb garden, and picnic areas are on the grounds.

❖ A. W. Hays Antique Truck Museum

200 East Main Street, Woodland 95695. (916) 666-1044. At I-5 and Road 102. Mon.–Fri., 8–4; weekends, 9–3. Closed holidays. Adults, $3; under 12, $1. Groups by reservation. W.

Junior (and senior) mechanics will find this a must-stop. There are 180 vintage trucks, in 120 different makes and models, from the turn-of-the-century truck with solid rubber tires to the beautiful 50s vintage hauler. The A. W. Hays museum is one of the largest collections of antique trucks in the world. This is a private, personal collection, and it's best to be there when A. W. himself can show you around, so call first.

❖ Old Sacramento

Sacramento was the major transportation hub for north-central California, providing a convenient location where water and land transportation systems could meet. Today, along the Sacramento River where Captain John Sutter established his Embarcadero in 1839, an important part of Sacramento's history has been restored to its former glory. Fifty-three structures built during the Gold Rush, including restaurants, stores, offices, and museums, stand as living memorials to their past. For tour information, call (916) 443-7815. Horse-and-buggy and covered-wagon rides are available.

The Old Eagle Theater at Front and J streets, which first opened in 1949, presents old melodramas and plays (box office: 916 446-6761; tours daily, 10–4; free).

The **Central Pacific Passenger Station** at Front and J streets (916 448-4466; 10–5 daily; free with Railroad Museum ticket) is a reconstruction of a station that was built in 1876. Waiting rooms, ticket offices, baggage rooms, and railroad cars tell their stories. This is where passengers board the hourly excursion trains on summer weekends.

The **Old Sacramento Schoolhouse** at Front and L looks just as it did in the 1880s (916 383-2636; Mon.–Sat., 9:30–4:30; Sun., 12–4:30; free).

The **B. F. Hastings Museum** at Second and J streets was the first western terminus of the Pony Express and the Sacramento office of Wells Fargo. Wells Fargo and Pony Express exhibits beguile, as do the reconstructed Supreme Court rooms, the Grass Valley stage, and posters on the early post office system. You can tap out Morse Code or write with a quill pen (916 445-4655; Tues.–Sun., 10–5; free).

The **Huntington-Hopkins Hardware Store**, a reconstruction of one of the West's more historic hardware stores, shows off old tools and supplies in a surprisingly appealing display (1111 I Street; 916 446-4466; Tues.–Sun., 10–5; free).

"Sacramento Illustrated" offers a 15-projector multimedia portrayal of Sacramento's history (925 Front Street; 916 638-0355; weekends, 12–6). A nominal fee is charged.

The **Sacramento History Museum** is an ultramodern portrayal of the Sacramento Valley from prehistoric times to the present. Docents are on hand to explain the exhibits, from the wall of pictures of Yosemite outings to the canning machinery that runs around you as you walk down the stairs (101 I Street; 916 264-7057; Tues.–Sun., 10–5; adults, $3; ages 6–17, $1.50; tours).

❖ Matthew McKinley Paddlewheel Excursion Boat

1207 Front Street, Sacramento 95814. (916) 552-2934. Call for prices and schedule.

This luxuriously appointed riverboat offers cruises for individuals and groups, from a renovated wharf in Old Sacramento. The cruise goes downstream past Miller Park, the old industrial wharves, and the Sacramento Yacht Club. The *Spirit of San Francisco*, once owned by John Wayne, still takes sightseers for a paddle-wheeling brunch, lunch, happy hour, or dinner dance.

❖ California State Railroad Museum

Second and I streets, Old Sacramento 95814. (916) 445-7387/448-4466. Groups: 445-4209. Adults, $5; ages 6–12, $2. Daily except holidays, 10–5. Groups by appt. W.

This state-of-the-art museum combines slide shows, theater presentations, panel exhibits, dioramas, interpretive exhibits, shiny locomotives, and historic railroad cars to walk in and around so you can see how trains have affected our history and culture. You start your self-guided tour with a movie—and then walk through the back wall of the theater into Gold Rush California. There wander through Lucius Beebe's elegant private car, the Railway Post Office Car, where you can sort mail, and the St. Hyacinthe Sleeping Car that really rocks; these three are highlights. Don't forget to see the toy and miniature train collection upstairs.

In summer, there are special hourly steam train excursions from the Central Pacific Freight Depot at Front and K streets (adults, $3; ages 6–17, $2).

✦ Crocker Art Museum

216 O Street (at Third), Sacramento 95814. (916) 449-5423. Wed.–Sun., 10–5; Tues., 1–9. Closed holidays. Ages 18–64, $2; ages 7–17 and over 65, $1. Tours for hearing or visually impaired. W.

The oldest art museum in the West was built around 1873 to house the paintings and prints collected by Judge Edwin Bryant Crocker. The collection includes pottery from the fifth century B.C. through contemporary works of art. Rococo mirrors, frescoed ceilings, and curving staircases make the building itself a work of art. Concerts, lectures, and other special demonstrations and events are scheduled throughout the year.

✦ California State Capitol

10th and Capitol, Capitol Mall, Sacramento 95814. (916) 324-0333. Daily, 9–5. Free. Guided tours on the hour. W.

After 13 years of construction, the State Capitol building was completed in 1874. It has recently been restored to its historic 19th-century dignity and beauty. It's fun to wander the halls and see the county window displays—and hear the rustle of politics in action.

✦ Old Governor's Mansion

1526 H Street (at 16th), Sacramento 95816. (916) 323-3047. Daily, 10–4, with tours on the hour. Adults, $2; ages 6–12, $1.

The official residence of California's 13 governors from 1903 to 1967 is now a handsome Victorian museum that captures the history of the state. The melange of furnishing styles reflects the different inhabitants. The old carriage house has been converted to a museum where you may view photographs, hats, fans, parasols, and memorabilia of the governors and their families.

❯❯ Visionarium

2701 K Street, Sacramento 95816. (916) 443-7476. Mon.–Fri., 10–4:30; Sat. until 5; Sun., noon–5. Over 15, $4.; under 15, $2.50. W.

The newest attraction for kids in Sacramento is this extremely popular hands-on museum.

❯❯ Sutter's Fort State Historic Park

2701 L Street (at 28th Street), Sacramento 95816. (916) 445-4422. Daily except holidays, 10–5. Adults, $2; under 18, $1. "Soundstiks" information wand free. Tours, groups, Environmental Living Programs, and demonstrations by appt. W.

Monica from Bitterwater Tally School wrote, "Dear Sutters Fort, Thank you for giving us the opportunity to participate in the ELP. It was fun looking at the rooms like the bakery, the kitchen, and the others. It was fun working there, too. I enjoyed it." Sutter's Fort is one of the best places to relive California history. The fort and its buildings and stables have been perfectly reconstructed, and the cooperage, doctor's office, candle-making room, kitchens, trading post, blacksmith shop, guard room, bunk room, and Sutter family quarters are all as they once were.

The songs and information provided through audio wands are clear, helpful, and entertaining. For example, while facing a model of James Marshall showing Sutter the gold he found at the mill, you hear their conversation and Sutter's German-Swiss accent. An orientation room in the museum relates Sutter's biography and the life of the California pioneers. A doll that survived the Donner party is on display. ELP enables fourth- to sixth-graders to actually spend a night at the fort, spinning wool, weaving baskets, and preparing their evening meal over fireplaces and in the beehive ovens. Living History Programs also allow youngsters of all ages to step back into the wild West.

❯❯ State Indian Museum

2618 K Street (between 26th and 28th streets), Sacramento 95816. (916) 324-0971. Daily except holidays, 10–5. Adults, $2; ages 6–17, $1. Films by request. Groups by appt. W.

This mesmerizing museum is a treasure house of the Native American world. Dioramas and well-labeled exhibits display Maidus grinding acorns, the healing child dance, headdresses, maps, minerals, musical instruments, games, jewelry, household goods, baskets, and featherwork.

Ishi, last of his California tribe, shows his Yahi way of life in photographs, in film, and on tape. Hands-on areas, such as a place to touch different pelts and a table for use of a mortar and pestle, add spice to the exhibits.

❖ Sacramento Children's Museum

1322 O Street, Sacramento 95814. (916) 447-8017. Weekends, 10:30–4:30 and by appt. Admission, $2; group discounts. Children must be accompanied by an adult. Call for schedule and prices of special programs and classes. W.

The Sacramento Children's Museum provides children with a vivid environment of discovery, learning, and problem solving. Hands-on learning programs, interactive exhibits, and participatory activities lead to explorations in art, architecture, nature, science, geography, and the humanities.

❖ Blue Diamond Growers

1802 C Street (at 17th), Sacramento 9814. (916) 446-8409. Mon.–Fri., 10 and 1, and by appt. Tasting room open 10–5 weekdays, 10–4 Sat. Video. Groups by appt. Free.

Franciscan fathers brought the almond from Spain to California in 1769. Today Blue Diamond is the world's largest almond packer. Visitors see the many unusual machines designed to sort, crack, halve, slice, dice, and roast almonds. You see concrete silos eight stories high, a mile-long conveyor belt, and an explanatory movie on the hour-long tour; then dig into the 12 different flavored almonds in the tasting room. Writes Christina: "The best part was when we got to talk on the phone. You were very nice to us. And I liked the free almonds. I liked the movie. I learned a lot from you about almonds."

❖ Fairytale Town

William Land Park, 1501 Sutterville Road, (off I-5). Sacramento 95822. (916) 264-5233. Daily, 10–4:30, except rainy days and Christmas. Ages 3–12, $2; 13–64, $2.50; over 65, $1. Combination tickets to Fairytale Town and the Sacramento Zoo are available at either gate.

Nursery rhymes and favorite stories come to life as children crawl through the Holes in The Cheese, skip along The Crooked Mile, sit in Cinderella's Pumpkin Coach, and slide down the circular slide after visiting Owl's House. You can visit the Three Little Pigs, Mary's Little Lamb, and The Tortoise and the Hare in Farmer Brown's Barn.

Children's birthday parties can be held in King Arthur's Castle (916 264-7061) and in Sherwood Forest daily except Sunday. Special events, such as Farmer Brown's hoedown or a scarecrow-stuffing contest, are held monthly. Puppet shows are given hourly on weekends and school holidays.

❖ Sacramento Zoo

William Land Park, 3930 West Land Park Drive, Sacramento 95822. (916) 264-5166. Daily except Christmas, 10–4. Adults, $3.50 weekdays, $4 weekends; ages 3–12, $2. There are strollers, wagons, and wheelchairs to rent. W.

Over 400 animals live in this tree-shaded garden and zoo. Any inhabitant of the reptile house is a favorite; others are the wallaroos, flamingos, giraffes, and the hippo. New orangutan, tiger, lion, and chimpanzee exhibits show these beautiful animals in natural settings. The new Rare Feline Center houses a Geoffroy's cat, jaguar, and margay.

❖ Sacramento Science Center

3615 Auburn Boulevard, East Sacramento 95821. (916) 277-6180. Wed.–Fri., 12–5; weekends, 10–5. Adults, $2.50; youth, $1.50.

Changing hands-on exhibitions focus on topics such as the human body and flight; a planetarium, outdoor Discovery Trail, and special events round out the visitor's experience.

❖ Silver Wings Museum

Mather Air Force Base, Building 3860, Rancho Cordova 95670. Off Highway 50, east. (916) 364-2177. Mon.–Fri., 10–4; weekends, 12–4. Free. W. Mather Air Force Base is scheduled to close in 1993, so call first.

Military and civilian aircraft displays and films dating from the Wright Brothers to Vietnam are presented in this reproduction of a 1914 hangar. There are World War I and World War II aviation displays, models, engines, and a remembrance of the pioneer women. The Teeny-Genie, an experimental pleasure plane with a VW engine, is super.

The Mather Planetarium in Rancho Cordova is open to groups by appointment. You'll see stars, planets, comets, meteor showers, outlines of constellations, and other space phenomena on a domed ceiling (916 364-2908).

❖ Nimbus Fish Hatchery

2001 Nimbus Road, Rancho Cordova 95670. On the American River. (916) 355-0666. Daily, 8–4. Free. W.

After fighting their way from the Pacific Ocean, salmon and steelhead spawn here each fall and winter. The hatchery has a capacity of 20-million salmon eggs and accounts for 60 to 70 percent of the commercial catch off the California coast. Visitors can see raceway ponds, the fish weir and ladder entrance, a holding pond, the sorting and spawning area, nursery ponds, and the hatchery building.

❖ Gibson Ranch County Park

8552 Gibson Ranch Road, Elverta 95626. Take Watt Avenue north to Elverta Road; left on Elverta to Gibson Ranch. (916) 991-9500/991-2066. Daily, 8–dusk. Fee per car, $5. Groups and tours by reservation. Call Mon. and Tues., 9–4. Picnic areas.

This 326-acre park is really a working farm. There are cows, hens, and horses to feed, and muskrats, ducks, and geese swim in the lake, which you can fish or swim in. There are ponies and horses to ride, paddleboats to rent, old buggies and a blacksmith shop to play with, and hayrides to enjoy.

❖ Folsom Project Dam and Powerplant

7794 Folsom Dam Road, Folsom 95630. (916) 989-7275. Tues.–Sat., at 10 and 1. Free.

Drive on top of the dam and past the gorgeous lake to get to the powerhouse. Tours pass three generators, with capacities of 66,240 kilowatts each, and go through the dam, depending upon how many people are visiting at the time.

❖ Folsom City Park and Zoo

50 Natoma Street, Folsom 95630. (916) 355-7200. Daily except Mon., 10–4. Free.

This small zoo specializes in Northern American native animals, with some exotic imports. Many of the animals were raised as pets; some are disabled. None can live wild. The zoo is located in City Park, which offers shaded picnic and barbecue areas and an extensive area of new playground equipment for both preschool and older children. A one-third scale steam train runs in summer and fall (916 355-7200).

Downtown, Historic Sutter Street has been restored to old buildings and shops that remind visitors of happier times. The Historical Society has opened the **Folsom History Museum** in the 1850s Wells Fargo Assay Office. The museum offers a slide show of local Indian and Gold Rush history and important local sites (916 985-2707). At Sutter and Wool streets, the reconstructed Southern Pacific Depot displays historical treasures.

Further out of town, the **Folsom Powerhouse**, on Riley Street, relayed electricity to Sacramento from 1895 to 1952. For tours, call (916) 988-0205.

❖ Western Railway Museum

Box 191, Antioch 94509. Rio Vista Junction, 10 miles east of Fairfield on Highway 12, 12 miles from I-80. (707) 374-2978. Weekends and holidays, 11–5. Adults, $4; ages 4–15, $2; under 4, $1.

The Western Railway Museum was put together by a nonprofit organization of men who love trains. You can walk through and around the more than 120 retired trolleys and steam locomotives or just watch the railroad buffs at work. An old-fashioned Salt Lake & Utah observation car is a favorite for dreaming (remember Judy Garland in *The Harvey Girls?*), as are the Birney "dinkey" streetcars, a New York City "el," a Pullman car that's been made up for sleep, a Toonerville trolley from the Key System, Oakland and San Francisco streetcars, and many more. The gift shop at the entrance holds the largest collection of railroad books in the West, along with cards, old ads, tickets, and badges. Picnic areas are available. Rides are frequent on weekends.

On weekends mid-March to mid-May, special excursion trains take visitors to the **Jepson Prairie**, the best unplowed stand of native bunch-grass prairie in the Central Valley, with vernal pools ringed with wild-flowers. Call for reservations and prices for these remarkable two-hour tours.

❖ Rio Vista Museum

16 North Front Street, Rio Vista 95471. (707) 374-5169. Weekends, 1:30–4:30 and by appt. Free.

All of the treasures in this little museum have been donated by local residents. There are antique etchings and photos; newspapers and books; and farm implements such as tools, plows, a buggy, a wagon, a forge, and a foundry, typewriters, a wine press, Chinese hats, and local birds' eggs. The museum was created during the Bicentennial, "so," says its curator, "we won't forget all about the past."

❖ Micke Grove Park and Zoo and San Joaquin County Historical Museum

11793 North Micke Grove Road, Lodi 95240. South of Lodi 3 miles, on Highway 99 and on Highway 5. Park: (209) 953-8800. Daily, dawn to dusk. On weekends and holidays, $3.50 per car. Rental facility reservations: (209) 953-8800/331-7400. Zoo: (209) 331-7270. Daily, 10–5. Adults, $1.50; children and seniors, 50 cents. Museum: P.O. Box 21, Lodi 95241. (209) 368-9154. Wed.–Sun., 1–5, and by appt. Free. Japanese Garden: daily, 9–2. Free. W.

This bustling community park offers picnic and play areas, the full range of water sports, a rose garden and a Japanese garden, horseback riding, nature trails, and party facilities. The museum, zoo, and amusement park are all near the main north entrance parking lot.

"Man and Nature Hand in Hand" is the theme for the remarkable multibuilding museum. In the main building, changing exhibits are always based on memories of the pioneer people, including a millinery shop and Victorian sitting room, both meticulously furnished. On the grounds, you can visit the Tree & Vine building, the Delta building, an 1800s Calaveras schoolhouse, a 1920s kitchen, a harness shop, a ranch blacksmith shop, a farm tools and tractor collection, a model of a dairy, and the Sunshine Trail Garden for the Blind. "Earth is so kind, that just tickle her with a hoe and she laughs up a harvest," is what one Delta farmer wrote, while another prophesied, "We will dig gold with a plow."

Lions, bobcats, gray foxes, kinkajous, pumas, and black leopards are some of the animals in this little zoo, now being refurbished. There are daily public feedings of the animals. The seal pool and tropical forest canopy always draw crowds.

❖ Pixie Woods

Louis Park, Stockton. Mail: City Hall, 415 North El Dorado, Stockton 95202. (209) 466-9890/944-8220. Fall and spring: weekends, 12–5. Summer: Wed.–Fri., 11–5; until 6 on weekends. Closed from Halloween to Easter Week. For those 12 and over, $1.25; under, $1. Train, boat, and merry-go-round, 50 cents. Parties by appt. W.

Stockton's fairyland is for the "young in age and young in heart." You enter the Rainbow Gates to a magical forest and enchanted lagoons and begin a journey that will take you through some of your favorite fairy-tale settings. Ride the Pixie Express or take a trip on the *Pixie Queen*, a replica of the paddle-wheel steamers that long ago graced the Delta waterways. And be sure to visit Pirates' Cove and the magical volcano. See a puppet show in the Toadstool Theater. Have an adventure in Frontier Town, and pet the animals in McDonald's Farm.

❖ The Haggin Museum

Victory Park, 1201 North Pershing Avenue, Stockton 95203. Off I-5. (209) 462-4116. Daily, except Mon. and holidays, 1:30–5. Donation. Groups by appt. W.

Three floors of history and art fill this handsome brick building. Interpretive displays of California and local history include an arcade of 19th-century storefronts, arms, a fire-fighters' gallery, and an American Indian Gallery. The Holt Hall of Agriculture includes a fully restored

1919 Holt 75 caterpillar tractor and a 1904 combine harvestor. The art galleries include work by American artists such as Albert Bierstadt. The letter by Daniel Boone, the Donner party relics, the port diorama, and the display of 100-year-old dolls are of special interest to kids.

➤ Miller Horse and Buggy Ranch

9425 Yosemite Boulevard, Modesto 95351. Take Highway 132 east 10 miles from Modesto. (209) 522-1781. Open "whenever Mrs. Mae Miller is there, which is most of the time." Reservations necessary. Call for current prices. One adult for every six children please.

This wagon collection and 1900 general store are fascinating, but they are so cluttered that some people may shy away. Those who climb in and poke around will be well rewarded. Over 50 cars and wagons, including stagecoaches, fire engines, beer wagons, racing sulkies, Victorian coaches, excursion buses, and an ambulance used in the 1906 San Francisco earthquake and fire are in the barn. A hurdy-gurdy and high-buttoned shoes, sausage stuffers, old typewriters, and a bicycle collection dating to the 1820s (including a mother-of-pearl tandem bike reputedly given to Lillian Russell by "Diamond Jim" Brady) are in the store.

➤ McHenry Museum

1401 I Street, Modesto 95354. (209) 577-5366. Tues.–Sun., 12–4. Free. Tours by appt. W.

"Not to know what happened before one was born is to remain a child," quoth Cicero. And that is the credo of this historical museum, which aims to appreciate the past and the people who pioneered this area. A complete doctor's office, a general store, a recreated blacksmith shop, gold mining paraphernalia, fire-fighting equipment, and a collection of guns and cattle brands are permanent exhibits. Changing displays focus on families, ethnic and religious groups, quilts, fans, dolls, and other areas of interest. Slide shows, movies, and musical events are held in the auditorium. And there are traveling exhibits to schools and groups.

Down the block, history buffs will want to visit **The McHenry Mansion**, which was built in 1883 and is one of the few surviving reminders of Modesto's past. Today the Italianate mansion has been completely restored and refurbished, right down to the William Morris–designed wallpaper, the rose brass gas chandelier in the front parlor, the 19th-century English wall-to-wall carpeting, and the newly milled redwood columns on the front veranda (906 15th Street at I, Modesto; 209 577-5341; open Tues, Wed., Thurs., and Sat., 1–4; group and individual tours and party rentals available; free).

More rambunctious kids will want to head for the new **Yes You Can** Children's Museum at 900 Third Street (209 521-1815), for hands-on educational entertainment.

❖ Castle Air Museum

Castle Air Force Base, P.O. Box 488, Atwater 95301. Off Highway 99 near Merced. (209) 723-2178. Daily except holidays, 10–4. Free. Shop and restaurant. W.

A B-24 Liberator bomber, its plexiglass bubbles bristling with machine guns and the bombs painted on its side numbering its World War II missions, greets you when you drive through Castle's gate. Volunteer enthusiasts refurbished this plane, along with the over three dozen military aircraft on view at the museum. There are bombers of all ages; jets; an up-to-date SR-71 spy plane; a plane so small a pilot can't fit in it; and one, a KC-97 Stratotanker, impossibly large. Air Force memorabilia in the indoor display such as a World War I machine gun, a top secret Norden bombsight, and a special display of NASA shuttle flights, add to little flyers' interest.

❖ Hershey Chocolate U.S.A.

1400 South Yosemite Avenue, Oakdale 95361. (209) 848-8126/847-0381. Mon.–Fri., 8:30–3, by appt. Visitors Center on G Street next to the park: weekdays, 8–5; Sat., 10–4:30. Free.

Once you register at the Visitors Center, you inhale and wait for the next available tour. Each visitor gets a coupon for a free chocolate bar. Then you're shuttled to the factory to see candy bars, chocolate kisses, and chocolate syrups made, weighed, packaged, and labeled in the course of a 30-minute tour. You pass huge chocolate vats, candy-bar molds in action, and rooms for the processing of instant cocoa and chocolate syrup. Then it's back to the Visitors Center for the fateful choice.

THE GOLD COUNTRY

To drive along Highway 49 is to relive California's history and legends. This is the Gold Country—the land of such writers as Mark Twain, Bret Harte, and Joaquin Miller, bandits like Black Bart and Joaquin Murietta, and heroes like Ulysses S. Grant and Horatio Alger.

Passing through little towns named Copperopolis and Jenny Lind, visitors who look carefully will see the traces of the hundreds of thousands of people—Cornish, Welsh, English, German, French, Italian, Mexican,

Peruvian, Australian, Chinese, and African—who migrated to this place seeking fame and fortune from the "tears from the sun." The town of Volcano still has an old Chinese store and a Jewish cemetery. In Gold Country, you'll find the only town in the United States ever to name itself a nation: Rough and Ready seceded from the Union in April, 1850, to become a republic with its own president, constitution, and flag. By the Fourth of July, it had slipped quietly back into the United States.

The many parks and campgrounds are mostly near quiet streams that once teemed with gold panners. Although there are mining, river rafting, ballooning, and kayaking expeditions available, to me, the best thing to do in the Gold Country is just explore, get a little lost. You'll have memorable experiences you couldn't possibly find listed in a book and you'll hear about towns that exist now only in history books. On the other hand, you could pick up a pan and start sifting....

❖ Railtown 1897—The Sierra Railway Company of California State Historic Park

Sierra Railway, P.O. Box 1250, Jamestown 95327. Off Highways 49 and 108 on Fifth Avenue, Jamestown. (209) 984-3953. Daily in summer, and on fall and spring weekends, 10–5. Adults, $4; seniors and youngsters, $2.50. Group rates. Varying times and prices for special train rides. Museum-gift store. W.

The Sierra Railway has been working since 1897 and been starring in movies since the Marx Brothers went west. After a short film, you'll be guided through the roundhouse to see rolling stock that's starred in over 200 films, from *High Noon, Petticoat Junction*, and *Wild Wild West* to *Mother Lode Cannonball* and *Butch Cassidy & the Sundance Kid*.

❖ Gold Prospecting Expeditions

Old Livery Stable, 18172 Main Street (P.O. Box 974), Jamestown 95327. (209) 984-GOLD. Call for details.

Every day, a tape showing Jamestown's history and how to prospect for gold—and the couple who walked into Ralph Shock's store in January, 1895, carrying in a shopping bag 11 pounds of gold nuggets that totaled $140,000—is shown free. There's a "slough" right on the main street of Jamestown for an instant panning experience. Families and groups can go on expeditions that take an hour or two days, by foot, river raft, or helicopter. Harlan of Modesto wrote, "Thank you so much for teaching me how to pan for gold. It could come in handy sometime. I enjoyed your explaining about gold and its uses. I also enjoyed panning for gold...."

✦ Tuolumne County Museum and History Center

158 West Bradford (P.O. Box 299), Sonora, 95370. (209) 532-1317. Mon., Wed., and Fri., 10–4; Tues., Thurs., and Sat., plus Sun. in summer, 10–3:30. Free.

This thriving museum is proud of its Gold Exhibit, which features the Tuolumne County Gold Collection—44 specimens including two solid gold nuggets. Information about the three gold rushes (in 1849, at the turn of the century, and currently, with open pit mining) is found in photos, lithographs of early mining scenes, and a large map showing where all the gold camps were located. Mark Twain memorabilia and vignettes tell the exciting story of Tuolumne County. Part of the museum is in the 1857 county jail, and you'll find an old bunkhouse in one jail cell and an extensive gun collection in another, with fascinating tales of the stalwart, independent men who used them. Bill West's cowboy paintings are popular with kids.

Two blocks west on Bradford and West Stockton Road is **Prospector's Park**, with a five-stamp mill, an authentic arrastre, and an impulse waterwheel, along with information plaques.

✦ Sonora Fire Department Museum

City Hall, 94 North Washington Street, Sonora 95370. (209) 532-4541. Daily, 10–4. Free.

Speaking trumpets from the 1850s, handmade uniforms from the 1870s, and leather firemen's helmets are displayed along with trophies and hand-operated fire-fighting equipment, including the Eureka No. 1, which was shipped around the Horn from New York in 1876.

Sonora, once called the Queen of the Southern Mines, is a well-preserved town. Visitors may be interested in stopping by at the Archaeology and History Display in the A. N. Francisco Building (48 West Yaney Street; free) to see bottles, fragments, and objects found on the site of the building during construction. Another display case contains memorabilia from the 1854 *Union Democrat*, including old type, photos, headlines, and old editions.

✦ Columbia State Historic Park

P.O. Box 151, Columbia district 95310. Highway 49, north of Sonora. (209) 532-4301. Daily except Christmas and Thanksgiving, 10–4:30. Free. W.

Columbia, "The Gem of the Southern Mines," is the best of the restored gold-mining towns. The streets and wooden sidewalks lead you to buildings, stores, and eateries outfitted as they were in the town's heyday.

The Columbia Gazette office, open to the public on weekends and all summer, still prints a small newspaper; the **Columbia Candy Kitchen** still sells hand-dipped candy; the 1857 **Douglas Saloon** still dispenses an occasional draft beer along with sarsaparilla.

Peek into the carpenter's shop and the schoolhouse, which has a bell tower, pump organ, desk, and potbellied stove. The Chinese herb shop, the fandango hall, the town jail, firehouse, blacksmith shop, and drugstore are other main attractions. Fallon House, a Victorian-era hotel, houses a repertory theater and ice cream parlor. The gold scales in the Wells Fargo Office weighed out over $55 million in dust and nuggets of the $87 million mined here. You can also ride a stagecoach and pan for gold!

During **The Hidden Treasure Gold Mine Tour** (209 532-9693; adults, $5; children, $2.50), visitors see the quartz vein that gold formed in millions of years ago and discover what "side drifts" and "glory holes" are all about.

The park museum offers slide shows and exhibits on the Indians, the Chinese population (once one-sixth of Columbia), and the gold miners. Your family could happily spend a day—or a weekend—in this thriving town of yesteryear.

✦ Moaning Cave

5350 Moaning Cave Road, Vallecito 95251. Off Parrots Ferry Road, between Columbia and Highway 4. (209) 736-2708. Daily 45-minute tours, 10–5 in winter, 9–6 in summer. Adults, $5.75; ages 6–11, $2.75; under 5, free.

You can count the 144 winding steps that lead you 165 feet down to a graveyard of prehistoric bones and moaning sounds. You'll see fantastic rock formations, such as Elephant's Ears and the Little Girl's Face, that add to the eerie feeling you're intruding on unknown spirits. The main chamber is tall enough to hold the Statue of Liberty. Stalactites hang "tight" from the ceiling and stalagmites are "mighty mounds" in the floor—that's how we remember which is which. Moaning Cave also offers a three-hour-long "Adventure Tour," with a 180-foot rappel, or rope descent, for ages 12 and up. Picnic tables with a view of the hills offer a pleasant spot to wait, as does the exhibit-filled waiting room.

✦ California Caverns

Cave City, Box 78, Vallecito 95251. Mountain Ranch Road, 9 miles east of San Andreas. Daily, 10-5, but not open if there's snow or rain. Hours depend on water level inside the cavern. (209) 736-2708. Adults, $5.75; ages 6–12 $2.75.

"When we emerged into the bright landscapes of the sun everything looked brighter, and we felt our faith in Nature's beauty strengthened, and saw more clearly that beauty is universal and immortal, above, beneath, on land and sea, mountain and plains in heat and cold, light and darkness." John Muir wrote this after wandering through the 200-foot-deep crystalline jungles. California Caverns offers an 80-minute "Trail of Light" tour and "Wild Cave" expedition tours for the adventurous.

❖ Mercer Caverns

P.O. Box 509, Murphys 95247. Ebbetts Pass Highway, 1 mile from Murphys. (209) 781-2101. Daily, 9–5 in summer, 11–4 on winter weekends and holidays. Last tour at 3:15. Adults, $5; ages 5–11, $2.50.

This 45- to 50-minute tour past stalactites and stalagmites, aragonites and helictites, takes you into a subterranean wonderland. Eerie rock formations like the Organ Loft, Angel Wings, and the Chinese Meat Market are dazzling examples of the artistry of nature. Mercer Caverns was discovered in 1885 by a tired, thirsty prospector, Walter J. Mercer, who noticed bay bushes growing near a limestone bluff and thought he had found a well. Stacey loved the story about Mr. Mercer, but "my favorite part was the beautiful formations that you turned into very wild fairy tales. I especially liked the Rapunzel story. It was so fantastic the way the limestone shaped itself into the shape of a girl with long hair. The little frog prince that was so embarrassed it turned around all the time was cute too."

❖ Angels Camp Museum

753 Main Street, Angels Camp 95222. (209) 736-2963. Daily, 10–3. Adults, $1; children, 25 cents. W.

A sulky, phaeton, surrey, hearse, steam tractors, and a mail stage are part of this extensive collection of antiques, clocks, old wagons, and rolling stock. Old mining equipment and the working stamp mill are especially fascinating. Indian artifacts and memorabilia of the county's past are nicely presented. Homage is paid to Mark Twain and the annual Jumping Frog Contest.

❖ Calaveras County Historical Museum

30 Main Street, San Andreas 95249. (209) 754-6579. Daily, 10–4. Adults, 50 cents; children, 25 cents. W.

The Hall of Records Building in the County Courthouse and Jail has been transformed into a beautifully designed treasure house. You can walk through the judge's chambers and then go downstairs to see the cell where

Black Bart awaited trial. The museum focuses on the Miwok way of life and on the people living in San Andreas during the 1880s, with representative rooms and exhibits.

✥ Amador County Museum
108 Church Street, Jackson 95642. (209) 223-6386. Wed.–Sun., 10–4. Donation.

Working scale models of the Kennedy Mine Tailing Wheel No. 2, the Kennedy Mine head frame, and a stamp mill, along with a gold room tracing the history of the area from the discovery of gold to the advent of the hard-rock machinery, and a "Congress of Curiosities"—almost an old-fashioned Sears Roebuck catalog come to life—make this cheerful museum a pleasant stop. The children's bedroom and the chair used by a woman while driving her own covered wagon west are personal favorites. A tape and live narration show one-half hour long shows how gold was mined.

One mile out of town on North Main Street there are two wheels on each side of the road, 58 feet in diameter. They were used to transport waste from the mine to a reservoir a half-mile away. Almost lost in history, the huge wheels are still impressive.

✥ Chaw'se Indian Grinding Rock State Historic Park
14881 Pine Grove–Volcano Road, Jackson 95689. East of Jackson 9 miles. (209) 296-7488. Day use: $5 per car; $4 for a senior's vehicle; $20–40 per bus. Museum open daily, 11–4 in winter, longer in summer. W.

At first, the huge flat limestone bedrock, 173 feet long by 82 feet wide, looks empty. But then you look closer and discover the petroglyphs scratched in by the Miwok Indians to commemorate their hunting and fishing tales. You'll also see the 1,185 mortar cups where the women ground the seeds, bulbs, fungi, and acorns that served as the staples of their diet. The acorn meal was sifted and washed many times to remove bitterness, then the meal was mixed with water in a basket and heated by hot rocks dropped into the mush. One family would consume 2,000 pounds of acorn a year. Visitors may also see a ceremonial roundhouse, a granary, eight bark dwelling houses, and a hand-game house.

✥ Chew Kee Store
Fiddletown 95629. Just off Highway 49 outside Plymouth on the way to Volcano. Daily in summer and on Sat. in winter, 12–4. Free.

Built in the 1850s, the Chew Kee Store is believed to be California's only surviving rammed-earth structure of the Gold Rush era. The small store is a remarkable example of history frozen in time, "a fly in amber," since Jimmy Yee lived there from 1913 to 1965 and didn't change a thing. It's still a Chinese herb store with ceramic rice crocks, gambling hall receipts, prayers, and two spare back rooms left just as they were when Dr. Yee, Jimmy's guardian, died. The devoted local history buffs who take care of the store will be glad to tell you about it.

❧ Daffodil Hill

From Fiddletown, take Shake Ridge Road 3 miles north of Volcano. (209) 296-7048. Mid-Mar. to Mid-Apr., 10–5 daily. Free.

Although the hill is open only when the daffodils are in bloom around Easter, this is worth planning for. The McLaughlins have planted about 300,000 daffodils in many colors, and between the flowers and the 11 peacocks walking around, have created an enchanted hillside.

❧ Sam's Town Americana Museum

Cameron Park, Highway 50 (P.O. Box 1030), Shingle Springs 95682. (916) 933-1662. Daily, 8 A.M.–9 P.M. Ages 8–69, $1; others free.

If you close your eyes or ignore the sawdust-laden dining rooms, game room, and Gay 90s store and go through the red velvet curtains, you'll discover a well-presented wax museum with 29 historical vignettes. These include Lillie Coit and her horse-drawn fire engine, Abraham and Mary Todd Lincoln, a millinery shop, a barbershop-with-quartet, Jenny Lind, Lillian Russell, and Huckleberry Finn.

Vintage vehicles and movie memorabilia, such as Charlton Heston's cage from *Planet of the Apes*, stand on the grounds, which has a super "old-town" facade.

❧ El Dorado County Historical Museum

100 Placerville Drive, El Dorado County Fairgrounds, Placerville 95667. (916) 621-5865. Wed.–Sat., 10–4; Sun., 12–4. Donation. W.

"Smokers and chewers will please spit on each other and not on the stove or the floor." This sign is one of many in this big old barn of a museum staffed by caring volunteers. There's an old cash register run by steel balls, lots of dolls, a Civil War viewing casket, two well-stocked country stores, Snowshoe Thompson's nine-foot skis, a surrey with a fringe on top, and lots more. Right outside the door a mammoth shaking table, for separating gold from ore, and a walk-in Shay engine No. 4 grab the kids' attention.

In town, check out the 1852 **Fountain-Tallman Soda Factory Museum,** at 524 Main Street (916 626-0773; Fri., Sat., and Sun., 12–4; donation). The factory made baking soda, not ice cream sodas.

❧ Hangtown's Gold Bug Mine Park

549 Main Street, Placerville 95667. North of downtown Placerville 1 mile, at the end of Bedford Avenue. (916) 622-0832. Daily. Free. Picnic areas.

A ghost of an old gold miner narrates the entertaining, educational audio tour of Gold Bug, the only municipally owned, open-to-the-public gold mine in the world. It was worked as recently as 1947. The longer shaft (a 362-foot-long tunnel) of the mine ends at an exposed gold-bearing quartz vein. The occasional drip of water rings in the cool, eerie silence of the tunnel.

Placerville was originally called Old Hangtown after the Hanging Tree in the center of town. In one week, two Englishmen found $17,000 worth of gold on the main street of town. It is said that the legendary "Hangtown Fry" originated here when a miner walked into a restaurant and demanded a meal that used the three most expensive ingredients at once: eggs, bacon, and oysters.

❧ Marshall Gold Discovery State Historic Park

Highway 49 (Box 265), Coloma 95613. (916) 622-3470. Museum: daily except holidays, 10–5; 10:30–4:30 in winter. Adults, $1. Park: 8–sunset. Picnicking: $5 per car. W.

"This day some kind of mettle found in the tailrace...looks like goald." A millworker noted this in his diary in January, 1848. The gold found changed the face of California—and America.

Sutter's Mill has risen again on the American River. Across the highway, a modern museum is dedicated to the discovery of gold and the lives of the gold miners. Maps, tools, mementos, and pictures are displayed against informational panels and dioramas. Films narrated by Hugh "Wyatt Earp" O'Brien bring history to life. On the grounds, follow a self-guiding trail to see the mill; a Chinese store; a mine; a miner's cabin furnished with corn, beans, a scale, a bible, and the miner in bed; a Mormon's cabin; an arrastre (ore crusher); and a town that's almost disappeared. If you feel lucky, bring your own gold pan and boots.

❧ Placer County Historical Museum

Gold County Fairgrounds, 1273 High Street, Auburn. (916) 889-4134. Tues.–Sun., 10–4. Adults, $1; ages 6–16 and over 65, 50 cents. Group tours: (916) 889-6500.

Old mining equipment and pioneer mementos recall the early days of Placer County. Artifacts from Auburn's former Chinese community, the assayer's office, Indian relics, and the 45-foot-long walk-through model mine are informative. The exhibits change regularly but center on the personality of the '49er.

Also on the grounds, at 291 Auburn-Folsom Road, is the **Bernhard Museum Complex**. Benjamin Bernhard's restored home, winery, and wine storage building are open for tours by volunteer docents. The admission ticket serves for both places.

❖ Griffith Quarry Park & Museum

Taylor and Rock Springs roads, Penryn 95663. (916) 663-1837. Weekends, 12–4. Free. Group tours: (916) 889-6500.

The Quarry in Griffith Park, a relatively new Placer County museum, displays material on the granite works, the Griffith family, and the area.

❖ Forest Hill Divide Museum

24601 Harrison Street, Foresthill 95631. (916) 367-3988. May–Oct., weekends, 12–4. Free. Groups: (916) 889-6500.

The history of the Foresthill and Iowa Hill divides is shown in exhibits featuring material on geology, prehistory, the Gold Rush, transportation, early business, recreation, and early fire fighting. There's a scale model of the local logging mill. And special rotating exhibits keep kids coming back for more.

❖ Golden Drift Museum

32820 Main Street, Dutch Flat 95714. (916) 389-2126. May–Oct., Wed. and weekends, 12–4. Free. Groups: (916) 889-6500.

Exhibits explain methods of mining, especially hydraulic mining, and show how railroading, especially the Central Pacific, has affected the local communities.

❖ North Star Mine Powerhouse Museum

Lower Mill Street (at Empire), Grass Valley 95945. (916) 273-4255. Daily in summer, 11–5. Adults, $2; children, $1. Donation. Picnic areas. W.

Built by A. D. Foote in 1875, this is the first completely water powered compressed-air transmission plant of its kind. The compressed air, generated by 10-ton, 30-foot Pelton waterwheels, furnished power for the mine. The museum houses photos, ore specimens, safes, dioramas and models of the mines, an assaying laboratory, and a working Cornish pump. The star of the show is the 30-foot Pelton wheel itself.

❖ Grass Valley Museum

Mount St. Mary's, South Church and Chapel streets, Grass Valley 95945. (916) 273-1928. Tues.–Fri., 12–3; weekends, 10–3. Donation. W.

A schoolroom, 1880s doctor's office, children's bedrooms, a lace collection, and a glass slipper collection mix with convent memories in this quaint museum.

❖ Empire Mine State Historic Park

10791 East Empire Street, Grass Valley 95945. (916) 273-8522. Daily except holidays, 10–5. Adults, $2; children, $1; under 6, free. Group tours. W.

Keeping alive the story of hard-rock gold mining and its significance in California's history, the Empire is the oldest, largest, and richest gold mine in the area. Many of the 16 stopping points along the mine's self-guided tour are in ruins, and the sites are being reconstructed. The William Bourn family "cottage" is furnished and also open for tours. Movies, films, and Living History Days will help excite your imagination so you'll think of the hundreds of Cornish miners who dug the 367 miles of tunnels, almost 11,000 feet deep, and the mules that pulled the ore trains through the tunnels. Enterprising souls will want to know that there's still gold there to be gotten.

To relive a bit of history, have a Cornish pasty at one of the bakeries in town. The miners called these meat and potato pies "letters from home." Grass Valley is another nicely preserved Gold Rush town. While browsing, you may want to see the homes of Lola Montez and Lotta Crabtree on Mill Street. Lola was a Bavarian singer, dancer, and king's favorite who fled to America in 1853 when her king fell from power. Lotta Crabtree was Lola's protégée and soon became famous, rich, and beloved by the American public. Lola's home is open to the public (daily, 12–4, free in summer).

❖ Nevada County Historical Society Museum

Firehouse No. 1, Main and Commercial streets, Nevada City 95959. (916) 265-5468. Daily in summer, 11–4. In winter: Mon., 1–2:30; Tues., 11–4; Thurs.–Sun., 11–4. Donation.

Located in one of the quaint town's most photogenic buildings, the museum has just been completely refurbished. Maidu Indian artifacts, relics of the Donner party, children's toys and books, a Chinese altar, showshoes for horses, a photograph of a miner with the image of himself as a 12-year-old appearing mysteriously on the film, and pioneer memories will fill the space.

Nevada City, the best of the gold-mining towns, is a thriving community with the feel of turn-of-the-century Gold Country. Walking along the small streets is a pleasure. Visitors may want to stop at the

Orey Victorian Tour House (401 North York Street; 916 265-9250), a pretty pink Victorian.

✤ Malakoff Diggins State Historic Park

North Bloomfield Star Route, Nevada City 95959. Northwest of Nevada City 16 miles on a crooked mountain road; begin with Route 49 and follow signs. (916) 265-2740. Museum: daily in summer, 10–5; weekends in winter, 10–4. Tours by appt. Camping and picnicking, $5 per car.

Many millions of dollars worth of gold poured from these huge hydraulic diggins, and a small sign tells visitors that there's still enough gold left here, and on other sites around the area, to mine $12 million annually for the next 50 years. This park is a silent monument to the hydraulic miners. The museum displays a model of the monitor used in gold mines and shows how hydraulic mining worked. Photos of the 2-mile Bloomfield tunnel, the 12-foot-long miners' skis, a portable undertaker's table, mementos of the Chinese miners, and an old-time bar and poker room are some of the highlights. Walkers can also see a drugstore, a general store, and a livery filled with wagons. Films round out the experience.

✤ Kentucky Mine Museum & Sierra County Historical Park and Museum

Highway 49 (P.O. Box 260), Sierra City 96125. North of Sierra City 1 mile. (916) 862-1310. Memorial Day–Sept. 30, Wed.–Sun., 10–5. Also weekends in Oct. Guided stamp-mill tour, $4; junior rate for tours, half price; 12 and under, free with parent. Museum: $1.

Among the Northern Mines, the Kentucky Mine is one of the earliest of the hard-rock type, dating between 1928 and 1933 with equipment dating back to the 1860s and 1880s. It is one of the only stamp mills in the area that is still operable with the original machinery intact. The informative guided tour begins at the opening of the mine and follows the gold milling process from beginning to end. The Pelton waterwheels still work, too! The museum constantly changes its displays on Sierra County's past, which include mining equipment, logging machinery, skis, clothing and household articles, local minerals, wildflowers, and other natural history items. There are also exhibits on the early Chinese and the Maidu Indians, and a schoolroom. Picnic facilities are available. Concerts are held in the outdoor amphitheater in July and August.

☙ Plumas-Eureka State Park Museum

310 Johnsville Road (off county road A-14), Blairsden 96103. (916) 836-2380. Museum: 8–4 daily in summer; weekends in winter when staff is available. Free. W.

Snowshoe Thompson used to carry 60 to 80 pounds of mail on his back over the Sierra in winter for the miners. A pair of his extra-long skis are displayed in this packed museum, along with hard-rock mining equipment, an assay office, models of a stamp mill and an arrastre, natural history exhibits, and pioneer life remembrances. The outbuildings are fun, too.

☙ Plumas County Museum

500 Jackson, Quincy 95971. (916) 283-6320. Summer: daily, 8–5; May 31–Oct. 14, weekends, 10–4. Free. W.

This living museum depicts local history with artifacts, lumbering and mining displays, and an outstanding collection of Maidu Indian baskets.

☙ Donner Memorial State Park

Donner Lake, P.O. Box 9210, Truckee 96162. (916) 587-3841. Daily, 10–12, 1–4. Adults, $2; ages 6–17, $1. W.

During the disastrous winter of 1846, a party of 89 tried to make it through the mountains to California. Only 47 people survived, and some of the survivors resorted to cannibalism. Man's conquest of the Sierra Nevada and the tragic story of the Donner party are told with relics, dioramas, pictures, and models and are combined with natural history in The Emigrant Trail Museum. The pedestal of the memorial to the Donner Party is 22 feet high—as high as the early snowfall that trapped them. Chinese railroad workers, the "Big Four" railroad tycoons, miners, and mountain men are also remembered here.

☙ Lake Tahoe

Lake Tahoe Visitors Authority, P.O. Box 16299, South Lake Tahoe 96151. (916) 544-5050. (800) AT-TAHOE. North Tahoe Visitors & Convention Bureau, P.O. Box 5578, Tahoe City 95730. (916) 583-3494. Road conditions: (800) 822-5977. Information: (900) 776-5050. Lake Tahoe *magazine lists camping, dining, sporting, and lodging information, and other services.*

Lake Tahoe is justifiably world famous for its crystal-clear water and beautiful setting. Visitors can ski, water ski, boat, bike, ride, swim (only in August unless you're a polar bear), surf, sun, golf, windsail, hike, and enjoy the forest wilderness and the exhilarating clarity of the air and sunshine.

Naturalist programs are given on summer weekends in the D.L. Bliss and Emerald Bay state parks and at Camp Richardson. The U.S. Forest Service **Taylor Creek Stream Profile Chamber** near Camp Richardson is part of the El Dorado National Forest Visitors Center (daily, 10–5). You can take one of the self-guided nature walks through a mountain meadow and marsh and even down into the chamber for a fish-eye view of a mountain stream. Recorded messages help identify the fish and plants in front of you.

Vikingsholm Castle, a 38-room Nordic fortress (Bliss State Park, P.O. Box 266, Tahoma 96142; 10–4 daily; 916 525-7277/541-3030 in summer) on Emerald Bay's southwest shore is open to the public.

The Ehrman Mansion, (Sugar Pine Point, Highway 89, Tahoma 96142; summer tours, 11–4, fee) is an outstanding example of turn-of-the-century Lake Tahoe architecture.

The **Gatekeeper's Log Cabin Museum** (130 West Lake Boulevard, Tahoe City 95730; 916 583-1762; daily, spring to fall) displays Washoe and Paiute artifacts, local minerals and fossils, and other Tahoe memorabilia.

On the lake, you can sightsee from the **Tahoe Queen's Glass Bottom Boat**. (For information, call 916 541-3364; June to Oct., 11 A.M., 1:30 and 3:55 P.M; noon daily in winter. Tickets for adults, $13; ages 11 and under, $6.) Or take the **M.S. Dixie**, a Mississippi paddlewheeler that shows you another view of the lake. (For information, call 702 588-3508/882-0786.) Other boats cruise the blue waters as well.

In summer, you can also take a balloon ride with Contempo-Airy Balloons (916 573-2453).

The **Lake Tahoe Historical Society Log Cabin Museum** (3058 Lake Tahoe Boulevard, or P.O. Box 404, South Lake Tahoe 96150; 916 541-5458; 10–4 daily in summer) features artifacts from Tahoe's early days. The **Western America Ski Sports Museum** features ski exhibits from 1860 to the present, vintage ski movies, and artifacts of Snowshoe Thompson (at the Castle Park exit of I-80; Box 729, Soda Springs 95728; 916 426-3313; Tues.–Fri., 12–4; Sat. and Sun., 11–5; free).

Venture to the Nevada side of the lake for a visit to the **Ponderosa Ranch** at Incline Village (100 Ponderosa Ranch Road, Incline Village, NV 89451; 702 831-0691; 10–5 daily in summer, weekends in spring and fall) to see the Cartwright Ranch House, Hoss's Mystery Mine, Frontier Town, an antique car and carriage museum, the Ponderosa barnyard, and other attractions.

But you'll always head back to the glorious lake, gouged from the crown of the Sierra during the Ice Age and named in the language of the Washoe tribe "Big Water."

 THE FRESNO AREA AND MADERA COUNTY

Some people think that Fresno exists only as a stopping-off place from San Francisco to Los Angeles, but it's a big, booming city. The trip to Fresno is four hours by car from San Francisco, but there are so many motels you can usually be assured of a room when you arrive. Surrounded by orchards and rich farmland, pretty lakes, and an impressive irrigation system, Fresno is also the gateway to Sierra National Forest and Sequoia, Kings Canyon, and Yosemite national parks. Hiking, skiing, spelunking, and wandering through groves of the largest living things on earth, the giant Sequoia redwoods, are all available within 40 minutes' drive. Closer to Fresno, seven lakes offer sailing, fishing, houseboating, waterskiing, and windsurfing.

➢ R. C. Baker Memorial Museum

297 West Elm, Coalinga 93210. (209) 935-1914. Mon.–Fri., 9–12, 1–5; Sat., 11–5; Sun., 1–5. Free.

"I enjoyed going to your museum in Coalinga. I liked the photos of the earthquake, I loved those boxing cards that were $100 a card. I liked the old cameras, and that 1928 one dollar bill. I thought the car there was neat. I bet that would cost a lot of money. I liked all the different kinds of barbed wire. Speaking of barbed, I thought the barber or dentist chair was neat. And the big fossil was awesome. The uniforms and the guns were radical. The counting machines were weird, but I liked them too. One of the things that I liked the most was the telephone booth. I enjoyed the different rooms with dolls. But the thing I liked most about your museum was everything. Your museum was the best museum I have ever went to. Keep up the good work." This is the recommendation of Brandon, a visitor from Akers Elementary School.

The remodeled R. C. Baker Museum, named in honor of a Coalinga pioneer, oilman, and inventor, shows both the natural and man-made history of Coalinga. Visitors to Coalinga will enjoy a drive nine miles north on Highways 33 and 198 past the Grasshopper oil pumps—oil-field characters painted in many colors to look like clowns, birds, and animals.

⇒ Tulare County Museum

2700 South Mooney Boulevard, Mooney Grove Park, Visalia 93277. (209) 733-6616. Fall and spring: Thurs.–Mon., 10–4. Winter weekends; 10–4. Summer: weekdays except Tues., 10–4; weekends, 12–6. Adults, $1, and children, 50 cents, or $2 per car.

"End of the Trail," the bronze sulpture by James Earl Fraser portraying a tired Indian on a pony—once the most copied piece of art in the world—is the star attraction at this lively museum spread throughout 11 buildings. That sculpture was first exhibited in San Francisco in 1915 at the Panama-Pacific Exposition. A one-room schoolhouse, newspaper and dental office, Yokuts Indian collection, and rooms from turn-of-the-century homes recreate the past. Furniture, clothes, cooking utensils, toys, baskets, World War I uniforms, and early farm machinery are also on exhibit.

The 143-acre park offers picnic arbors and oak trees, boating, skateboard tracks, and more.

⇒ Tulare Historical Museum

444 West Tulare Avenue (P.O. Box 248), Tulare 93275. (209) 686-2074. Thurs.–Sat., 10–4; Sun., 12:30–4. Donation. W.

"Take a trip back in time" is the theme of this historic museum. You're greeted at the door by a life-size horse and doctor's buggy, then step back to a Yokuts village around Tulare Lake. Walk through the coming of the railroad, the lives of some of the early settlers, the three great fires that swept Tulare during its first 14 years, and the incorporation of the city. Minireplicas of rooms in an early Tulare home and local businesses revivify a time gone by.

⇒ Boyden Cavern

Kings Canyon National Park, Highway 180, 77 miles east of Fresno. (209) 736-2708. P.O. Box 78, Vallecito 95251. June–Sept., daily, 10–5; May and Oct., daily, 11–4. Adults, $5; children, $2.50; seniors, $4.50.

A 45-minute tour takes you into a wondrous world deep beneath the 2,000-foot-high marble walls of the famous Kings Gates. Massive stalagmites, delicate stalactites, and splendid arrays of crystalline formations defy description. Boyden Cavern is in the deepest canyon in the United States.

⇶ Clovis Big Creek Historical Museum

401 Pollasky Avenue, Clovis 93257. (209) 297-8033. Thurs. and Fri., 11–3; Sat., 10–4. Donation.

Artifacts from the first families of Clovis help make the past understandable in the present. There are Clovis High School pictures from 1918 to 1964. Youngsters are particularly fascinated by the flume that swept lumber to Shaver Lake.

⇶ Porterville Historical Museum

257 North D Street, Porterville 93257. (209) 784-2053. Thurs., Fri., and Sat., 10–4; and by appt. Free. W.

The main room of the museum, a former Southern Pacific Railroad Station waiting room, houses an interesting collection of Yokuts Indian baskets and other artifacts along with a collection of mounted birds and animals. Cattle industry memorabilia, including cattle brands, barbed wire, and saddles and tack, are in the Wilcox Room. A graciously furnished turn-of-the-century bedroom is the latest addition. Vignettes of the drugstore, dentist's office, lawyer's office, and kitchen are well done. A doctor's office is in progress.

⇶ Zalud House

393 North Morton (at Hockett), Porterville 93257. (209) 784-1400 ext. 461. Wed.–Sat., 10–4; Sun., 2–4. Adults 50 cents; children, 25 cents. Groups by appt. W.

One of the state's unsung treasures is this remarkably preserved and lovingly cared for Victorian home. Pearle Zalud was born in 1884 and lived there until her death in 1970. Her world tour at age 19 was the first of many, and the home bears the beautiful fruits of her worldwide souvenir hunting. The house is exactly as she left it—which is exactly as her father liked it in 1912, when her mother died. The art and furnishings, the hats, dolls, and collars and laces, the framed antique valentines, and the family photos all create a house that is a home.

Third-grader Carrie wrote, "Thanks for taking us through the Zalud House. It was fun. Some people say that it is haunted but I don't think it is because it is beautiful. And I wish that I lived there."

Porterville is lucky enough to have been given not only the house and its contents but also an extremely able and caring curator who has spent years documenting and cleaning all the the Zaluds' belongings. These include linens and clothing bought half a century ago and never taken out of the original boxes, and such pantry supplies as a 1909 can of baking powder and a 1912 old gas stove that still works. The curator really enjoys sharing this world with visitors, and children love the story of Pearle's brother Edward, a cowboy who was killed while riding, and her brother-in-law William, who was shot to death by a woman in the Porterville Pioneer Hotel in 1917. The chair with the bullet hole is upstairs.

Since there was so much left in the closets, the curator changes the exhibits in the rooms with the seasons. The beautiful flower gardens outside are available for private parties and weddings. Videotaped oral histories and films are sometimes shown.

⫸ Colonel Allensworth State Historic Park

Sotourna Avenue, Allensworth. On Highway 43, 20 miles north of Wasco; on Highway 99, 9 miles west of Earlimart. (805) 849-3433. Daily, 10–4:30. Parking fee, $3. Camping available. To schedule a tour, write: Star Route 1, Box 148, Allensworth 93219.

The only California town to be founded, financed, and governed by black Americans is being restored to its 1908 state. A Visitors Center with exhibits and films, picnic area, and two museums, the colonel's residence, and the original schoolhouse are open to the public upon request, as is the 15-unit campground. The Mary Dickinson Memorial Library is open now, along with the Morris Smith House and the Hinsman Family Home, which is open to overnight guests who want to experience living in the past.

⫸ Lindsay Olive Growers

650 West Tulare Road (P.O. Box 278), Lindsay 93247. Take Route 65 to West Hermosa, West Hermosa to Westwood, Westwood to Tulare Road. (209) 562-3082. Mon.–Fri., 10–4. Groups by appt. Free. W.

Did you know that a single large black olive has 4.54 calories in it? Lots of calcium? And no cholesterol? Visit the Lindsay Olive factory showroom and watch a 20-minute film "tour" about the history of the olive and California with tips on how to grow, pick, and cure olives, while you taste to your heart's content. Tools and olive-wood crafts are displayed.

⫸ Pioneer Village Museum

Art Gonzales Parkway (adjoining Highway 99), Selma. Mail: 1814 Tucker, Selma 93662. (209) 891-2320. Weekends, 9–4; weekdays, 8:30–5; also "seasonal hours." Adults, $2; seniors, $1.50; children, 50 cents. Groups by appt. W.

Victorian homes and cherished buildings are being moved to, and restored in, this museum-in-progress. Visitors walk through a museum store and out on the grounds to a 1904 Victorian Queen Anne, the old barn built by a Civil War veteran, the Ungar Opera House, Selma's 1887 Southern Pacific Depot, and a 1901 Little Red School House, steepled church, doctor's office, barber shop, pottery shop, and newspaper office.

❖ Fort Roosevelt Science Center

870 West Davis (P.O. Box 164), Hanford 93202. (209) 582-8970. By appt. only. Adults, $1.50; children, $1. Overnights and birthday parties.

Local businesses and families have worked with the California Department of Fish and Game to set up this natural history museum and rehabilitation center. The museum itself is in the 1893 Hanford Railroad Freight Depot. There's an old two-story log cabin, covered wagons, a windmill, and a water wheel by the pond. There's an adopt-an-animal program, and on-site educators really get the youngsters involved with the world around them.

❖ Kearney Mansion & Kearney Park

7160 West Kearney Boulevard, Fresno 93706. Kearney Park, 7 miles west of downtown Fresno. (209) 441-0862. Fri.–Sun., 1–4. Adults, $3; ages 13– 17, $2; under 12, $1. Groups by appt.

Built between 1900 and 1903, the restored home of M. Theo Kearney, pioneer Fresno land developer and raisin baron, has preserved many of the original furnishings, including European wallpapers, art nouveau light fixtures, and replicas of original carpets and wallpapers.

❖ Discovery Center

1944 North Winery Avenue, Fresno 93703. Take Highway 9 to McKinley, then east to North Winery Avenue. (209) 251-5531. Tues.–Sun, 11–5. Adults, $1.75; ages 5–16, $1. Group rates. Summer science camp and astronomy program. Picnic areas and playgrounds. W.

This hands-on science center helps children try things out for themselves. There's a bubble machine, a tree that lights up by sound, a feel box, a reaction machine, a laser beam, pipe phones, and a peripheral-vision tester. The Indian room has a Yokuts hut and shows the many things that Indians have introduced to civilization. Dioramas of the animal and vegetable life of the valley and streams are also fun to look at. Children have a great time here.

❖ Fresno Arts Center

2233 North First Street, between Clinton and McKinley avenues, Fresno 93703. (209) 485-4810. Tues.–Sun., 10–5. Adults, $2; $1 for students and seniors. Weekends free. W.

A forum for the arts of the 19th and 20th centuries, with revolving exhibits, classes, planned tours, and lectures.

❯ Meux Home Museum

1007 R Street at Tulare (P.O. Box 70), Fresno 93707. (209) 233-8007. Fri.–Sun, 12–3:30. Adults, $3; ages 13–17, $2; ages 5–12, $1. Groups by appt: 209 431-1926.

The docents in this sweet blue-and-white Queen Anne enjoy talking about Victorian family life and explaining how things worked back when. Special events like the Teddy Bears' picnic make this a class favorite. Indeed, Fresno schoolchildren were some of the many contributors to the refurbishment of this elegant family home. A plaque thanks them for the sponsorship of the breezeway in the kitchen area. Visitors enjoy Dr. Thomas R. Meux's Confederate uniform and surgical tools as well as his portrait in a Rhett Butler mustache, and the clothing, jewelry, wedding gowns, and photographs. There are also storytelling afternoons and a gift shop.

The nearby **German Museum** (3233 North West Avenue; (209) 229-8287; Mon.–Fri, 12–4; 9:30–12 on Sat., free; W), run by the American Historical Society of Germans from Russia, offers lectures, workshops, and discussions about the art, literature, and folklore of their forefathers.

❯ Fresno Metropolitan Museum of Art, History and Science

1555 Van Ness Avenue, Fresno 93721. (209) 441-1444. Wed., 11–7, free; Thurs.–Sun., 11–5. Adults, $3; seniors $2; students, $1.50. Tours by appt. W.

Explore art, history, and science in the San Joaquin Valley's largest museum. The Met features a permanent hands-on center of science and art with 40 interactive exhibits. In this "playground for the mind," children can weave a web of lightning from their fingertips, walk away from their shadows, and become strong enough to bend light. The museum also has a permanent exhibition devoted to award-winning author William Saroyan, including his 1942 Academy Award. In a room full of Yosemite stagecoaches and wagons, you can read eyewitness accounts such as this man's, from 1884: "...we tried all possible devices to steady ourselves, and to avoid concussion of the spine, which really appeared inevitable...at last we entered the true forest belt and anything more beautiful you cannot conceive. We forgot our bumps and bruises in sheer delight. Oh the loveliness of the pines and cedars...."

⇒ Fresno Zoo, Storyland & Rotary Playland

894 West Belmont Avenue, Roeding Park, Fresno 93728. Freeway 99 between Olive and Belmont. (209) 264-5988. Zoo: over age 14, $4; 4–14, $1. Daily in winter, 10–5; until 6:30 in summer. W. Groups: 488-4440. Storyland: $2.50 for those over 3. Spring and fall weekends and holidays, 10–5. Closed Dec. and Jan. May 1–Labor Day, 10–5. Playland: 486-2124. Prices and hours vary depending on season; usually, 10 to 5 when school's out. Boating costs also vary.

The Fresno Zoo is one of the most progressive in the country. In the South American Tropical Rain Forest Exhibit, visitors walk through a lush habitat of free-flying birds and small primates. The computerized state-of-the-art reptile house has been extremely successful in breeding almost-extinct animals. The elephants thrive in the waterfall and deep pool in their section. Winding paths and lush foliage add to the pleasure of a stroll through the zoo, as does the "Ask Me!" cart program. Kids especially like meeting hawks and owls face to face when the docent takes them out of their cages for discussions with visitors.

In Storyland, talking storybook keys ($1.75) persuade the blue caterpillar to tell eight classic fairy tales. Then when children have heard the stories, they can go on to visit the heroes of the tales. They can play in King Arthur's castle, Red Riding Hood's Grandmother's cottage, or Mr. Toad's cart, or they can talk to Simple Simon's pie man, the knaves of Alice's court, or Little Miss Muffet and Winnie the Pooh.

Children will find Rotary Playland irresistible. There's a roller coaster, a Ferris wheel, a kiddie car ride, a scenic miniature train ride, and a merry-go-round. Paddle boats, motor boats, and rowboats to rent by the hour on Lake Washington attract the seaworthy, and there are concessions and picnic areas.

Fort Millerton, also in the park (weekends, May 1–Sept. 30, 1–4; donation), houses a small exhibit of pioneer life, with antique toys, lumber tools, and the medical kit of Fresno's first doctor.

⇒ San Joaquin Fish Hatchery

Friant, 93626. Off Highway 41, 13 miles northeast of Fresno. (209) 822-2374. Daily, 8–4:30, except 7:30–4 in summer. Free.

There are more fish in this one spot than you'll ever see again: more than two million trout in sizes that range from pinhead to fingerlings ready to catch are raised in these trout-hatching ponds. Four times a day the fish are fed high-protein dry pellets. When they're a year old and 10 inches long, they're taken in tanks by plane and truck to the heavily fished lakes and streams of California. But while they're here, it's really fun to walk along the 48 ponds and watch the fish leap over and slide down the little dams between them. A photo exhibit explains about trout habits and the trout-seeding program.

California's Fish Hatchery and Planting Program runs 22 hatcheries, most open to the public. Call your local Fish and Game Department office for information on the one nearest you.

❯❯ Friant Dam & Millerton Lake State Recreational Area

P.O. Box 267, Friant 93626. Off Highway 41, north of Fresno. (209) 822-2332. Daily, daylight hours. Park entry, $6 per car.

Fed by Sierra snows, the waters of Millerton Lake are released into the Friant-Kern and Madera irrigation canals to feed the rich croplands of Fresno and Madera counties. The dam is 319 feet high and 3,488 feet long, with a reservoir capacity of 520,000 acre feet. You can walk halfway across the dam while guides tell you the history of the project. The old Millerton Courthouse, overlooking the dam, is a pleasant little museum of Friant history (by appointment: P.O. Box 205, Friant 93626; 209 822-2332).

❯❯ Madera County Museum

210 West Yosemite (P.O. Box 478), Madera 93637. (209) 673-0291. Off Highway 99 from Fresno. Weekends, 1–4 and by appt. Free.

Patrick wrote: "Thank you for letting us come. I saw a lot of interesting rooms. I saw a lot of great ones. The best ones are mining, store, parlor, saloon, war and peace, native Americans, and downtown." Three floors of displays in this 1900 granite courthouse emphasize the county's mining, logging, and agricultural history. The section of flume from the Madera Sugar Pine Lumber Company is overwhelming. The "downtown" room shows what the city looked like in 1900 and even has a stagecoach in which people rode to Yosemite Park.

❯❯ Sierra Mono Indian Museum

P.O. Box 275, North Folk 93643. At the intersection of Roads 225 and 228, off Highway 41 from Fresno toward Bass Lake. (209) 877-2115. Mon.–Sat., 10–4, and by appt. Adults, $2; high schoolers and seniors, $1.50; grade schoolers, 75 cents. W.

The only Indian museum in California solely owned and operated by an Indian tribe without any outside help, the Sierra Mono Indian Museum is a triumph of care, hard work, and attention to detail. The dioramas of

wildlife in nature and vignettes portraying Indian foods and culture
are well labeled and beautifully designed. Did you know that rattlesnakes
are born alive, not hatched from eggs? You can see some unborn baby
rattlesnakes if you look carefully. The museum offers classes and demonstrations on basketmaking, beadwork, acorn gathering, and other arts
and crafts.

❯❯ Fresno Flats Historic Park

*School Road, Oakhurst. School Road is Road 427; off Highway 41. (209)
683-6570/683-7766. Tues.–Sat., 1–3; Sun., 1–4. Costumed docents host
groups. For appt., write to SHSA, P.O. Box 451, Oakhurst 93644. Free.
Picnic Area.*

Designed to capture the flavor of family life in Central California's
foothills and mountains a century ago, Fresno Flats is preserving buildings
along with memories. The old Fresno Flats school is now a museum with
interesting artifacts and revolving exhibits, but the Laramore-Lymon
1878 farmhouse and the 1869 Taylor log house are living museums. A
jail, blacksmith shop, old barn, wagon-stage collection, and flume are also
on the grounds. One side of the Taylor log house is furnished as a late-
19th-century living room, and the other contains the re-creation of an
early-day forest ranger's office, complete with maps, old tools, and a display on how the house was constructed.

❯❯ Mariposa County History Center

*P.O. Box 606, Mariposa 95338. At 12th and Jessie, off Highway 49.
(209) 966-2924. Daily, 10–5; weekends only in winter. Donation.*

In what proud Mariposans call "the finest small museum to be
seen anywhere," you'll see a typical miner's one-room cabin with all his
worldly possessions; the more comfortable home of the West's most famous explorer, John C. Fremont, and his wife, Jessie; a street of shops
reminiscent of the 1850s; a one-room schoolhouse; and art and artifacts
showing how gold was formed and extracted. Of special interest are the
"Dear Charlie" letters posted throughout—letters written by Horace
Snow in 1852 through 1854 to Charlie, his boyhood friend in Cambridge,
Massachusetts. They give a miner's-eye view of life in the mines more
than a century ago. The five-stamp mill, Indian Village with bark houses,
sweathouse, and mining exhibits on the grounds are also worth seeing.

The Mariposa County Courthouse is the oldest courthouse still
in use in California (10th and Bullion streets; 209 966-3222; in winter,
Mon.–Fri., 9–5; Apr.–Oct., on weekends; and by appt.; free). The clock in
the tower has been marking time since 1866.

❖ California's State Mining and Mineral Exhibit

P.O. Box 1192, Mariposa 95338. Mariposa County Fairgrounds, near Highways 140 and 49. (209) 742-7625. May 1–Oct. 31: Mon.–Sat., 10– 6; Sun. 1–4. Winter: Wed.–Sun., 10–6. Adults, $3.50; seniors and students 5–13, $2.50. Group rates: 209 742-7625.

The 20,000-piece collection flourishes on a hillside where '49ers once mined the gold-rich ore. There are 100 Mother Lode gold specimens, an assay office, mining equipment, models for hands-on experiences with stamp mills, and picnic spots for all. In the central gallery, the dramatic crystals and brightly colored minerals star in the "Golly, gee-whiz" section. Outside, you can walk through a 200-foot mine tunnel showing veins of gold ore and various mining techniques, such as drilling, blasting, and mucking, in progress. The gift shop has fabulous crystals and minerals for sale along with books and fossils.

❖ Yosemite Mountain Sugar Pine Railroad

56001 Yosemite Highway 41, Fish Camp 93623. (209) 683-7273. Adults, $6–$9; children, $3–4.50.

Just four miles from Yosemite National Park's south entrance, this narrow-gauge steam railroad operates on a restored section of old logging rails for a four-mile narrated trip through magnificent forest scenery. Model A railcars operate daily, April through October; steam trains run May through October. Special winter runs are also available. Moonlight specials include a barbecue dinner and music around the campfire. An 1856 log cabin is the site of the Thornberry Museum with artifacts and photos of the logging era. Food service and gifts are available at the station. Call or write for complete schedule. Boarding assistance is offered for handicapped persons. Groups and parties are welcome.

❖ Yosemite National Park

Enter through Fish Camp on Highway 41, at El Portal on Highway 140, or on Highway 120 (this road to Tioga Pass is closed during the winter, which may last until May). Visitors Center: (209) 372-0265. Center open daily: in summer, 8–6; 9–5 in spring, fall, and winter. Museums open daily. Cars, $5 a week if staying outside the park.

If you and your family had only one sight to see in California, your best choice would be Yosemite National Park. Yosemite is one of the world's wonders, a world within itself. Elevations range from less than 2,000 feet to over 13,000, and in these 11,000 feet, five different plant belts exist. Each sustains a part of the park's wildlife population of 220 bird and 75 mammal species. In this natural splendor, you can hike, swim, camp, fish, ski, ride horseback or burro, bicycle, or simply wander.

Your first stop should be the Visitors Center in Yosemite Valley, where you can learn about the park from the center's pamphlets, exhibits, audio-visual programs, lectures, and guided walks. *The Yosemite Guide*, free, at entrance stations, gives the latest schedules. There are fireside programs for youngsters (summer only).

Where you go in Yosemite will, of course, depend on your time, interests, and the season. You can choose from mountains, giant sequoia groves, towering waterfalls like Bridalveil, and sites with breathtaking vistas of Sentinal Rock and El Capitan.

There are also museums in Yosemite for rainy days or a change of pace. The **Indian Cultural Center**, near the Visitors Center, is of interest (daily, 9:30–12, 1–4). Be sure to go through the self-guiding reconstruction of the **Ahwaneechee Indian Village**, which is open at all times. During the summer, there are cultural demonstrations in the Indian Village. At the **Pioneer Yosemite History Center** at Wawona, you can wander through a collection of horse-drawn vehicles, an old jail, a miner's hut, a working wagon shop, and a covered bridge. In the summer, old-time crafts demonstrations of soap-making, rail-splitting, and spinning are fun, and you can talk to costumed historian-interpreters who portray the original occupants of the cabins representing the different stages in the development of Yosemite National Park.

The Yosemite Travel Museum in the administration area near the Arch Rock entrance, tells the story of early-day railroad and auto tranportation in the region. It has a caboose, a locomotive, and a couple of cars on the grounds. The **Geology Museum** at the Visitors Center in Yosemite Valley shows how the mountains, waterfalls, and gorges were formed. The natural history of the area is also explored at the **Happy Isles Nature Center**, which is youth oriented, with summer Junior Ranger programs, dioramas, and interactive displays.

Yosemite By Air is one way to see it all. One-and-one-half-hour tours leave from Fresno Air Terminal (adults, $109; ages 2–12, $69). Call or write, but be sure to reserve in advance (800 622-8687, 209 251-7501; 4885 East Shields Avenue, Suite 201, Fresno 93727).

Yosemite is overcrowded in summer, so aim for other times, if possible. For information about the park, write to Superintendent, Yosemite National Park, CA 95389, or telephone (209) 372-0200. Camp reservations may be made through Ticketron, or call (209) 372-0307. Hotel reservations are a must. Call (209) 252-4848 or contact Yosemite Park & Curry Co., Yosemite National Park 95389. For road and weather information, call (209) 372-0300. For recorded general information, call

(209) 372-0265; live, 372-0265 (9–5, weekdays). For a brochure on access for disabled visitors, including special programs, parking, free shuttle bus service, guides, restrooms, and more, call (209) 372-0200 or write to Accessibility Coordinator, P.O. Box 577, Yosemite National Park 95389. All facilities and services are listed in the quarterly *Yosemite Guide.*

✦ Bodie State Historic Park

Bodie is 13 miles east of Highway 395, 7 miles south of Bridgeport. Mail: Friends of Bodie, P.O. Box 575, Bridgeport 93517. Museum open Memorial Day–September 30, 10–5. Park open Memorial Day–Labor Day, 9–7; 9–4 or as posted the rest of the year. There are no facilities. Not accessible in winter. Admission, $5 per passenger vehicle, $40 per bus. Smoking in parking lot only.

Nestled high in sagebrush country, Bodie, the largest ghost town in the West, has escaped all the commercialism often found in ghost towns. The 170 original buildings that still stand are maintained in a state of arrested decay—neither restored nor allowed to decay further. You walk by the 1878 Methodist church, the windowless jail, a frame schoolhouse, a small home that belonged to President Herbert Hoover's brother, the morgue with caskets still on view, and the iron vault of the bank. Information comes from a self-guiding tour pamphlet ($1), stowed, in summer, at the entrance station. Just wander through this quiet, ramshackle town and imagine all the high adventures that occurred here, more than a century ago. As Mark Twain wrote, "The smoke of battle almost never clears away completely in Bodie."

 NORTH CENTRAL CALIFORNIA

The north-central to northeastern area of California is the most rugged, remote section of the state, offering many unique and extraordinary sights. Lava Beds National Monument, Modoc National Forest, and Lassen Volcanic National Park are snowed-in in winter and blazingly hot in summer. Distances between towns are long, so be sure to arrange overnight camping or lodging before you set out. Nature lovers will enjoy the Whiskeytown–Lake Shasta–Trinity area and McArthur Burney Falls Memorial State Park—and all the wonderful open spaces whose inaccessibility leaves them unspoiled.

✦ Community Memorial Museum

Butte House Road, Yuba City 95991. From Sacramento take Highway 99 north, turn left in Yuba City at the 99/20 intersection, then turn right at

Civic Center Boulevard and right onto Butte House Road. (916) 741-7141. Tues.–Fri., 9–5; Sat. and Sun., 12–4. Free. W.

This small community museum uses local artifacts—from baskets and grinding pots to antique pianos and dishes—to celebrate and explain the life and times of Sutter County. Experience life in Sutter County from the first Maidu Indian inhabitants and the settlement of John Sutter at Hock Farm to the "civilization" of the county, and its agricultural development. Changing exhibits reflect the diverse interests of Sutter County today. Eight-year-old Tasha's "favorite thing was Lola Montez's dressing table," and her schoolmate, Anay, liked the player piano and blacksmith's tools.

➤ Beale Air Museum

Beale Air Force Base, Marysville 95901. From Sacramento, take Highways 99 and 70 north to Marysville. Turn east on North Beale Road and continue 10 miles to the base's main gate; tell the guard you're visiting the museum. From the gate, follow signs 5 miles to the museum. (916) 634-2516. Tues.–Sat., 9–4. Free. W.

Parked outside the museum are planes that reflect Beale's role as a base for bomber and reconnaissance flights. These include a B-25 light bomber and an A-26 light bomber. A U-2 spy plane sits in front of the base headquarters. Inside the museum, you can check out Air Force memorabilia from six decades: World War II survival kits, including silk escape maps, leather helmets from the 1930s, and modern fiberglass helmets with attached oxygen masks.

A vintage B-29 nose section protrudes from the back of the museum's second floor—and visitors are welcome to crawl through it. They can also sit inside a C-47 or peek into a T38 with an open canopy to see all the instruments close up. A World War II ambulance spotlight, a Russian T55 tank, and an AT-11 bomber trainer are some of the other treasures given immediacy by the reenactors, people in World War II costume who give tours. The theater shows military films, such as stealth films and Desert Storm footage, and Hollywood movies from World War II classics to *Top Gun* and *Memphis Belle.*

➤ Mary Aaron Memorial Museum

704 D Street, Marysville 95901. (916) 743-1004. Tues.–Sat., 1:30–4:30 and by appt. Free.

Warren P. Miller built his crowned gray and white Gothic family home for $5,000 in 1857. Today it is a museum with period furniture and clothing and an interesting display of dolls, documents, and photos. Our favorite: the 1860s wedding cake that was discovered perfectly intact and petrified in a wooden Wells Fargo storage box. The bricked garden has Victorian wrought-iron furniture and plantings.

On the levee of the river, the **Bok Kai Temple**, an 1879 Chinese temple for the River God of good fortune, houses many cultural artifacts (on D Street; 916 742–ARTS; by appointment).

❧ Sacramento Valley Museum

1495 E Street (Highway 20 at I-5), Williams 95987. (916) 473-2978. Apr.–Nov.: Wed.–Sat., 10–4; Sun., 1–4. Winter: Fri. and Sat., 10–4, and by appt. $1. Picnic area. W.

The 21-room museum has captured the past with a fully stocked general store, a blacksmith shop and saddlery, an apothecary shop, a barbershop, and restored early-California rooms filled with memories. The double cradle from the 1700s is special. The fashion doll collection is a history of civilization from ancient Greek times to the 1930s. In the document room, there's an 1800 newspaper reporting George Washington's death.

❧ Oroville Chinese Temple

1500 Broderick, Oroville 95965. (916) 538-2496. Fri.–Tues., 11–4:30; in summer, also Wed. and Thurs., 1–4. Ages 12 and over, $2. In groups, by appt., $1.50.

This complex of Buddhist, Taoist, and Confucian temples houses one of the finest collections of Chinese artifacts in the United States. At the door of one building stands a two-ton, cast-iron urn given to the temple by Emperor Quong She. Carved teakwood altars, old tapestries, gods and goddesses, dragons, rare lanterns, and shrines decorate the buildings. The Moon Temple, used for Buddhist worship, is entered through a circular doorway, which symbolizes the circle of life. The arts and lives of the thousands of Chinese who migrated to the gold fields are reflected in this peaceful spot. One young visitor wrote, "I enjoyed when the dragon was playing with the Moon. And the room where I saw the big guardians at the door and the big swords."

❧ Judge C. F. Lott Historic Home in Sank Park

1607 Montgomery Street, Oroville 95965. (916) 538-2497. Fri.–Tues., 11–4:30; also 10–4 on Wed. and Thurs. in June, July, and August. Over 12, $2. In groups by appt., $1.50.

"I like the courting chair because I think it was neat that the father got to know the daughter's fiance. I also liked the kitchen and the bride's room and the guest room." A fourth-grader from the Camptonville Elementary School wrote this in her thank-you note. This sweet Victorian has a lot of love in it—from the plaque in the front trellis that says "In commemoration of a kiss and a promise given between these columns" to the semiprecious stones from the local riverbed spelling out "Love" in the front parlor. Visitors of all ages will walk through authentically furnished rooms and learn what it was like to live in the late 19th and early 20th centuries.

The **Oroville Pioneer Museum**, further up Montgomery Street at number 2332, is a grand collection of pioneer memorabilia including early typewriters, an old fire engine, and pictures of the Oroville floods, housed in a replica of a miner's cabin (P.O. Box 1743, Oroville 95965; 916 534-0198/534-8700; Sun., 1–4, and by appt.; closed July and August, December and January; donation).

The Butte County Historical Society is scheduled to open **The Ehmann Home** (1480 Lincoln Street, Oroville 95965; 916 533-5316; W; donation) on weekends and by appointment. This furnished Colonial Revival home features displays from the society's collection of historical artifacts and a gift store specializing in Ehmann-brand olives.

✢ Feather River Fish Hatchery & Oroville Dam

5 Table Mountain Boulevard, Oroville 95965. (916) 538-2222. Hatchery, daily, 8–6. Dam overlook (538-2219), daily except major holidays, 9–6. Free.

A large window in the hatchery enables visitors to see the salmon climb the fish ladder to spawn (usually) in September to October. Over 10,000 salmon and steelhead make their homes here. Ten miles up the road, you can get a good view of the 770-foot dam across the Feather River.

✢ Bidwell Mansion

525 The Esplanade, Chico 95926. (916) 895-6144. Daily except holidays, 10–5. Tours lasting 45 minutes, every hour on the hour, 10–4. Adults, $1.

Rancho del Arroyo Chico, covering 26,000 acres, was purchased in 1849 by agriculturalist and politician John Bidwell. His large Victorian home soon became the social and cultural center of the upper Sacramento Valley. Bidwell's is a California success story. He arrived in California in 1841, worked as a clerk for John Sutter, rose to the rank of general in the Mexican War, and then on July Fourth, 1848, struck it rich at Bidwell Bar. He set himself up at Chico and built a model farm. He raised corn, oats, barley, peaches, pears, apples, figs, quince, almonds, walnuts, wheat, olives, and casaba melons. He was elected state senator and congressman, and even ran for president. Visitors may walk through the graciously furnished rooms. Children will like the cabinet of stuffed birds in the general's office, Annie Bidwell's telescoping organ in the attic, and the intricate Victorian hair wreaths in the parlor. Bidwell Park, fourth largest municipal park in the nation, is also part of the Bidwell estate.

The **Stansbury Home**, an 1883 Italianate Victorian nearby at Fifth and Salem that's filled with period furnishings, is remarkable because only Stansburys have lived in it and it has never been remodeled or modernized (916 895-3848/343-0442; weekends, 1–4 and by appt.; donation).

❖ South Shasta Lines

G. A. Humann Ranch, 8620 Holmes Road, Gerber 96036. Holmes Road is 2 miles south of Gerber. (916) 385-1389. Open Sun. in Apr. and May, 12– 4. Adults, $4; under 12, $3.

A 1/4-inch scale model railroad based on the Southern Pacific, Gerber to Dunsmuir, under construction for 42 years, is now finished. There are 16 steam-type locomotives and 100 freight and passenger cars on 900 feet of track. There are 1,500 miniature trees, 1,000 people, and hundreds of animals on this detailed miniature system. In addition, a real steam locomotive takes visitors for a mile-long ride. A steam and gas antique farm machinery museum is also on hand.

❖ William B. Ide Adobe State Historic Park

21659 Adobe Road, Red Bluff 96080. North of town 1 mile. (916) 527- 5927. Park open 8:30–5 for picnics and fishing. Adobe open 12–4 or whenever the ranger is on hand, and by appt. Parking fee, $3. W.

"He hereby invites all good and patriotic citizens in California to assist him—to establish and perpetuate a liberal, a just and honorable government, which shall secure to all civil, religious and personal liberty." So wrote William B. Ide to introduce the Bear Flag Republic to California. As first president of the Bear Flag Republic, he brought California into the Union. But when the Republic failed, Ide went to the gold fields and then returned home to his adobe, which also served as a ferry station between Sacramento and Shasta's northern gold mines. The house is small and unassuming, with family photos, cradle and high chair, a furnished kitchen, and an unusual sleeping platform under the eaves. A smokehouse and a carriage house, with covered wagons, buggies, and Ide's branding equipment, are also open to the public. Two 300-year-old oaks mark the way to another small museum that includes gold-mining tools, an old button collection, and a well-used cribbage board. The Visitors Center display panels help the exhibits.

In Red Bluff, the **Kelly-Griggs House Museum**, 311 Washington Street, is open for old-house buffs. The fence around the house is made from bars of the old jail (916 527-1129; Thurs.–Sun, 2–5; donation).

➣ Salmon Viewing Plaza

Lake Red Bluff Recreation Area, North Central Valley Fishery Resource Office, P.O. Box 667, Red Bluff 96080. Exit I-5 at Antelope Boulevard and follow Antelope Boulevard west to first stoplight, which is Sale Lane. Continue on Sale Lane 2 1/5 miles to the plaza. (916) 527-3043. Daily, 6 A.M.–10 P.M. Free.

Visitors may see, on TV monitors, king salmon on their way past fish ladders to upstream spawning grounds at the Salmon Viewing Plaza near the Diversion Dam in the Red Bluff Recreation Area. They can also see fish trapping, from an elevated walkway. The site is self-guided with several interpretive displays. The best time to visit is September and October.

The U.S. Fish & Wildlife Service also operates the **Coleman National Fish Hatchery** 20 miles away, next to the Battle Creek Wildlife Area on the boundary between Shasta and Tehama counties. From I-5 take the Balls Ferry Road exit in Cottonwood and go east on Balls Ferry Road (Route 1, Box 2105, Anderson; 916 365-8622; Mon.–Fri. except holidays, 8–4; free). Here chinook salmon eggs are spawned daily in October, less frequently in November, December, and January.

➣ Yreka Western Railroad

P.O. Box 660, Yreka 96097. 300 East Miner Street, just east of I-5 via the Central Yreka exit. (916) 842-4146. Three-hour-long excursions depart at 10 A.M., Wed.–Sun.; on weekends only in September and October; also, limited winter holiday schedule. Adults, $10; children, $5. Reservations required.

Established by the local citizenry in 1889 to link Yreka with the Southern Pacific tracks, the local short-line railroad has been in continuous operation ever since. The Blue Goose excursion train now brings new pioneers brave enough to be carried by Ol' No. 19, a boot-shined black 1915 Baldwin steam locomotive, through the Shasta Valley into Montague, with a one-hour stop in a quaint 1887 Southern Pacific depot/museum. Bandits have been known to attack the train to snatch bags of "gold" away from the kids—and replace them with candy.

❧ Carter House Natural Science Museum

Caldwell Park, 48 Quartz Hill Road, Redding 96003. (916) 225-4125. Tues.–Sun., 10–5. Adults, $1; children, 50 cents.

Did you know that tarantulas enjoy walking along your arm? In the animal discovery section of this lively science museum, you can pet a tarantula—or an opossum or ground squirrel. Native animals that are injured—sparrow hawks, screech owls, California king snakes—and domestic animals are cared for here. Programs such as hikes and science classes keep the place busy. Annie wrote, "Dear Carter House Museum. Thank you for telling us about animals. I liked learning about birds best. I learned that birds have beaks and bunnies don't."

❧ Redding Museum and Art Center

Caldwell Park, 56 Quartz Hill Road, Redding 96003. (916) 225-4155. June–Aug.: Tues.–Sun., 10–5. Sept.–May: Tues.–Fri., 12–5; Sat., 10–3. Closed holidays. Free. W.

Pomo Indian basketry, from cradles to pots, dresses, and luggage, and from houses to gifts for the funeral pyre, is one of the excellent exhibits in this well-organized center. The permanent Indian and primitive collections include Wintu Indian baskets, beads, and tools and focus on the history of the Shasta County area. The art galleries offer changing exhibits of contemporary artists and collections.

❧ Waterworks Park

151 North Boulder Drive, Redding 96003. (916) 246-9550. Memorial Day to Labor Day; call for times and prices. Group rates and team nights.

Beat the heat and cure those summertime blues with the wildest wettest time of your life. Three giant twisting, turning, serpentine water slides, a 400-foot wild white-water inner-tube river ride, a children's aquatic playground with fountains, pool, and slides, and water volleyball, picnic grounds, and games add up to a great vacation day.

❧ Fort Crook Museum

Fall River Mills 96028. (916) 336-5110. Northeast of Redding 75 miles on Highway 299 East. Daily, 12–4. Closed Nov. 1–May 1. Free.

There are six little buildings, including an 1884 one-room schoolhouse, in this historical museum, where artifacts reflect the history of the area. Old farm machinery, buggies, an old fire hose, baskets, a dugout canoe, and dolls all attract youngsters.

❧ Shasta State Historic Park

*P.O. Box 2430, Old Shasta 96087. Highway 299, west of Redding. (916)
243-8194. Thurs.–Mon., 10–5. Adults, $2; children, $1. Picnic areas near
the stagecoach and pioneer barn.*

Once the center of the rich northern gold mines, Shasta is a quiet
almost-ghost town now restored. The old county courthouse contains a
remarkable collection of California art along with displays of photographs
and relics of the Indians, Chinese, gold miners, and pioneers who once
lived here. Modoc handicrafts, Chinese wooden pillows and money, an
1879 *Godey's Ladies Book*, and the pistol John Brown used in his raid at
Harper's Ferry are among the highlights. The courtroom is furnished as it
was when in use, and the jail is still equipped with chains, leg irons, and a
gallows. The Litsch General Store, open in summer, looks just as it did in
the 1880s, with barrels of meat and wine, old hats, and picks and shovels
for sale. Within the park are the ruins of what was once the longest row of
brick business buildings north of San Francisco, the town's Catholic cemetery, and other sites that are fun and safe to explore.

❧ J. J. (Jake) Jackson Memorial Museum and Trinity County Historical Park

*P.O. Box 333, Weaverville 96093-0333. 508 Main Street, Highway 299
West. (916) 623-5211. Daily, May–Oct., 10–5; Apr. and Nov., 12–4.
Donation.*

Clear displays trace Trinity County's history from the days of the
Indians through the gold-mining years. Ray Jackson's collection of antique firearms, Chinese tong–war weapons, and a reconstructed miner's
cabin, stamp mill, and blacksmith shop help to recall this bygone era.

❧ Weaverville Chinese Joss House

*P.O. Box 1217, Weaverville 96093. Main Street, Highway 299 West.
(916) 623-5284. Daily except holidays, 10–4. Closed Tues. and Wed.,
Nov. 1 to Feb. 28. Adults, $1; children, 50 cents. Tours every hour on the
hour in winter, on the half-hour in summer.*

The Temple of the Forest and the Clouds is open for worship now, as
it has been since 1853. A small museum offers Chinese art, mining tools,
weapons used in the tong wars, and photos of Chinese laborers building
the railroads. A Lion Dance headdress, an abacus, opium pipes, and a huge
gong are also shown. Inside the temple, you see the paper money that is
burned for the gods and the drum and bell that wake the gods so they'll

hear your prayers. In the rear of the temple, the attendant's quarters are furnished as they were hundreds of years ago, with bunk beds and wooden pillows. Colorful altars, temple saints, celebration drums and flags, and the mirror-covered king's umbrella that guarded him against evil spirits create a vivid picture of what to many is another world.

✦ Ironside Museum
Hawkins Bar, on Highway 299 West near Burnt Ranch. Mail: Star Route Box 3, Hawkins Bar 95525. (916) 629-2396. By appt. Donation.

Ray Narchand shares his personal collection "whenever anyone wants to see it—if we're home." Pioneer artifacts include butter churns, doctors' instruments, a collection of 200 padlocks, a glass insulator collection, Mrs. Narchand's carnival glass collection, and high-button shoes. Assaying equipment, a stamp mill, a 10-foot waterwheel and a Little Pelton waterwheel, mining equipment, and a blacksmith shop share the bill with a complete dentist's outfit. If you call before your visit, Mr. Narchand will bring out his gun and gold collections, too. Kids are especially fascinated by the shoe horn and key collections.

✦ Shasta Dam
Highway 15 off I-5. Mail: 14225 Holliday Road, Redding 96003. (916) 275-1587/244-1554. Daily, 8–4. Visitors can drive or walk on the dam at any time. Information center, 9–5 daily. Tours by appt. Free.

Deer come to be fed by hand when the lights shine on Shasta Dam at night. During the day, the 602-foot dam, second highest in the world, is an even more spectacular sight. Snow-capped Mount Shasta (which the athletic can climb) looms in the distance, accentuating the differences between natural and man-made wonders. Jet-boat tours, camping, houseboating, and every kind of water sport are popular in this Shasta-Whiskeytown-Trinity National Recreation Area.

✦ Lake Shasta Caverns
P.O. Box 801, O'Brien 96070. Off I-5 on Shasta Caverns Road. (916) 238-2341. Tours hourly, 9–4. Adults, $12; ages 4–12, $6.

Discovered in 1878 by J. A. Richardson (you can still see his inscription), the Lake Shasta Caverns are a natural wonder. Stalactite and stalagmite formations range from 8 inches to, in the Cathedral Room, 60-foot columns of stalactite draperies that are studded with crystals. Multicolored formations unfold before you during your tour, as you hear geological facts and Wintu Indian legends from a knowledgeable guide.

⤜ Siskiyou County Museum

910 South Main Street, Yreka 96097. (916) 842-3836. Summer: Mon.–Sat., 9–5. Winter: Tues.–Sat., 9–5. Free.

In this reproduction of the Callahan Ranch Hotel, one of the first stage stops in Siskiyou County in the 1850s, visitors learn the story of Siskiyou County from prehistoric days to the present. On the mezzanine, you'll find a parlor, bedroom, children's room, and office complete with an antique switchboard. A schoolhouse, blacksmith shop, church, 1856 pioneer log cabin, ore car, and logging skid shack are situated in the 2 1/2 acre Outdoor Museum. Among the buildings is a replica of the Denny Bar Mercantile Company, the first chain store in California. Period merchandise is sold during summer months.

⤜ Lava Beds National Monument

P.O. Box 867, Tule Lake 96134. Off Highway 139. (916) 667-2282. Camping: $5 in summer, free in winter. Monument headquarters: 8–6 in summer, 8–5 in winter. Closed Thanksgiving and Christmas.

"Thank you for letting us go to the Lava Beds. I really enjoyed it. The reason skull ice cave was my favorite cave is because of the ice at the end. My second favorite was Hopkins Chocolate. That's because it's long and narrow." So wrote Michelle about her visit.

Natural and Indian history vie for visitors' attention in this monumental landscape of lava formations. The area abounds with natural wonders, including cinder cones that reach up to 500 feet. There are about 200 lava tube caves that can be explored with care. Some caves hold Modoc drawings that date back centuries. Captain Jack's Stronghold, formed of natural lava fortifications, is a grim reminder of later history: In 1872, Captain Jack led a band of Modoc Indians in an unsuccessful revolt against the U.S. Cavalry, which was ending their world. This was the only major Indian war in California and is not something Americans should be proud of. A short visit to monument headquarters will help you understand the geology, natural history, and past events of the area.

⤜ Alturas Modoc County Historical Museum

P.O. Box 1689, Alturas 96101. 600 South Main Street. (916) 233-6328. May 1–Oct. 31: Mon.–Sat, 10–4; Sun., 1:30–5. Donation. W.

To learn more about Captain Jack (see preceding entry) and see pictures of him, go to this pleasant museum in the far corner of the state. There are beads, baskets, arrowheads, and other artifacts of the Pit River, Paiute, and Modoc tribes, along with pioneer memorabilia. The collections of mounted animals and birds and antique guns are popular with visitors.

❖ Roop's Fort

P.O. Box 321, Susanville 96130. 75 North Weatherlow Street. (916) 257-3292. May 1–Oct. 31: daily, 10–4. Free. W.

Lassen County memorabilia, farming and lumbering machinery, artifacts of the Native Americans, and remembrances of the first settlers fill this interesting museum. You can peek through the logs of Roop's Fort to see how this emigrant store must have looked in 1854. Many wagon trains stopped here. Susanville is named after the daughter of Isaac Roop, governor of the Provisional Territory of Nevada and Nataqua. Historic murals are being painted all over town, including one of Susan and her father on Lassen Street.

❖ Lassen Volcanic National Park

Highway 36, Mineral 96063. (916) 595-4444. Information centers at Manzanita Lake and Sulphur Works are open 8–4 daily from June to late September. Road closed in winter.

Among the attractions in this rugged area are hot springs, boiling pools, mud pots, sparkling lakes, and the cinder cone that erupted in 1851. An Indian lore program at Manzanita Lake Visitor Information Center presents the story and customs of the Native Americans who once lived here. Other programs are scheduled irregularly. During the pioneer programs, naturalists use covered wagons to show how people lived when they were on the Nobles Immigrant Trail. Subway Cave, north of Manzanita Lake on old Highway 44 toward North Birney, just outside the park, is also worth a trip.

One note of warning: The grounds and thermal areas are treacherous, so keep hold of your children at all times. Lassen Peak erupted for seven years beginning in 1914 and it's still considered active. Remember, the hydrothermal caves are named Devil's Kitchen, Sulphur Works, and Bumpass Hell for good reason.

❖❖ January

Bear River Trail Riders Annual New Year's Day Ride, Bear River Lake Resort

San Francisco Sports and Boat Show, Cow Palace

San Mateo Auto Show, Fairgrounds

Harlem Globe Trotters, Oakland Coliseum

Winter's Eve at Chaw-Se State Historic Park

Golden Gate Kennel Club All Breed Dog Show, San Francisco

Four-Dog Sled Races, Prosser Lake and Donner Lake

Whale Watching begins, Point Reyes National Seashore

Fiddlers Contest and Crab Cioppino Feed, Cloverdale

❖❖ February

Sutter Creek Doll, Toy, & Miniature Show

Chinese New Year's Celebration, San Francisco

National Road Show, Oakland Coliseum

Crab Festival, Crescent City

Crab Feast, Bodega Bay

Redwood Region Logging Conference, Eureka

Chinese Bomb Day, Bok Kai Festival, Marysville

Cloverdale Citrus Fair

Clam Beach Run, Trinidad

Carnival and Spring Fair, Lakeport

California Special Olympics Water Games, Sonora

❖ March

Daffodil Hill Blooms, Volcano

Snowfest, Lake Tahoe

Camellia Show, Santa Rosa

Crab Feed, Ukiah

Draggin' Wagons Dance Festival, Sonora

Sierra Dog Sled Races, Sierra City, Truckee, and Ebbetts Pass

Candlefishing at Night, Klamath River

Fresno Camellia Show

Junior Grand National Livestock Expo, Cow Palace, San Francisco

Jackass Mail Run, Porterville

Sacramento Camellia Festival

❖ April

Log Race, Petaluma River

Fisherman's Festival, Bodega Bay

Baseball season opens

Annual Trinidad Crab Feed

Gem & Mineral Show, Cow Palace, San Francisco

Yacht Parade, Redwood City

Annual Trail Days, Bothe–Napa Valley State Historic Park

Clovis Rodeo

Great Duck Race, Sutter Creek

Carmel Kite Festival

Gold Nugget Days, Paradise

Children's Lawn Festival, Redding

Red Bluff Romp and Rodeo Roundup

Tea and Musicale, vintage cars display, Anderson Marsh State Historic Park

Pebble Beach Concours D'Elegance

Stockton Asparagus Festival

Coalinga Water Festival

Nikkei Matsuri Festival, San Jose

Apple Blossom Festival, Sebastopol

Fresno Folk Festival

Rhododendron Festival, Eureka

Boonville Buck-a-Roo Days

Calaveras County Jumping Frog Jubilee, Angels Camp

Motherlode Dixieland Jazz Festival

❖ May

Laguna Seca Races, Monterey

Cinco de Mayo Festivals in San Francisco and San Jose

Opening Day Yacht Parade, San Francisco

Ione Homecoming Picnic, Parade, & Carnival

Avenue of the Giants Marathon, Garberville

Bay to Breakers Race, San Francisco

Luther Burbank Rose Festival, Santa Rosa

Mendocino Art Fair and Whale Festival

Living History Days, Petalume Adobe State Historic Park

Native American Cultural Day, Anderson Marsh State Historic Park

Mt. Folk Festival, Potter Valley

West Coast National Antique Fly-In, Watsonville Airport

Bok Kai Festival & Parade, Marysville

Salinas Valley Fair, King City

Sacramento Jazz Jubilee

Dixieland Monterey Jazz Festival

Calaveras County Fair and Frog Jumping Jubilee

West Coast Relays, Fresno

Roaring Camp Mining Company Gold Prospecting Days

Chamarita Festival and Parade, Half Moon Bay and Sausalito (Pentecost Sunday)

Old Settler's Day, Campbell

Fireman's Muster, Columbia

Lamb Derby Days, Willow

Miniature Horse Show, Amador County Fairgrounds

Russian River Wine Festival, Healdsburg

Stump Town Days and Rodeo, Guerneville

Coarsegold Rodeo, Madera County

Fiddletown Gold Country Hoedown

Prospector's Daze, Willow Creek

❖❖ June

Black Bart Celebration, Redwood Valley

Sonoma/Marin Fair, Petaluma Fairgrounds

Upper Grant Avenue Street Fair, San Francisco

Fly-In and Moonlight Flight, Porterville

Alameda County Fair, Pleasanton

Merienda, Monterey's birthday party

Gualala Whale Festival

Fort Bragg Whale Festival

San Antonio Mission Fiesta, Jolon

Springfest, San Mateo Fairgrounds

Old Auburn Flea Market

Italian Picnic and Parade, Sutter Creek

Klamath Salmon Barbecue

Shasta Bridge Jamboree, Redding

Malakoff Homecoming, Nevada City

Solano County Fair, Vallejo

Novato County Fair

Pony Express Days, McKinleyville

Garberville Rodeo and Western Celebration

Father's Day Kite Festival, San Francisco

Bear Flag Day, Sonoma

Tuolumne Jubilee, Tuolumne City

Kit Carson Days, Jackson

Butterfly Days, Mariposa

Cornish Miner's Picnic, Grass Valley

Fiddler's Jamboree, Railroad Flat

Bonanza Days, Gilroy

Redwood Acres Fair, Eureka

Western Daze, Fairfield

Western Weekend, Novato

Vaquero Days, Hollister

Horse Show and Rodeo, San Benito

Midsummer Music Festival, Stern Grove, San Francisco

Highway 50 Wagon Train, Placerville

Secession Day, Rough and Ready (June 27)

San Francisco's Birthday Celebration

Russian River Rodeo and Sumptown Days, Guerneville

Truckee-Tahoe Air Show

❖ July

Old Time Fourth of July Celebration, Columbia

Old-Fashioned Fourth, Mt. Shasta

Old-Fashioned Fourth, Crescent City

San Jose America Festival

Napa County Fair, Calistoga (July Fourth)

Willits Frontier Days (July Fourth)

Hoopa Fourth of July Celebration, Hoopa

Salmon B-B-Q, Noyo

Sonoma County Fair, Santa Rosa

C.B. Radio Convention, Eureka

Bach Festival, Carmel

California Rodeo, Salinas

Nihonmachi Street Fair, Japantown, San Francisco

Asian Festival, Oakland Museum

Christmas in July Jazz Band Festival, Sutter Hill

Pony Express Celebration, Pollack Pines

Arcata Salmon Festival

Mendota Sugar Festival

Garberville Rodeo

Folsom Rodeo

San Mateo County Fair

Woodminster Music Series, Oakland (through September)

San Francisco Fair and Exposition

Hangtown Festival, Placerville

Sacramento Water Festival

Dune Daze, Samoa

Grand Comedy Festival, Eureka

Fortuna Rodeo

Water Carnival, Monte Rio

Jeepers Jamboree, Georgetown to Lake Tahoe

Fiesta Rodeo de San Juan Bautista

Captain Weber Days, Stockton

Obon Festival, Monterey

Obon Festival, Fresno

Scotts Valley Days

Gold Rush Jubilee, Callahan, Siskiyou County

Feast of Lanterns, Pacific Grove

Orick Rodeo

Roaring Camp '49er Day (July 22)

Gasket Raft Races

Turtle Races, Cloverdale

Nightboat Parade, Lakeport and Clearlake Highlands

Marin County Fair, San Rafael

Amador County Fair

❖ August

Old Adobe Days, Petaluma Adobe State Historic Park

Monterey County Fair

Humboldt County Fair, Ferndale

Dipsea Race, Mill Valley

Nihonmachi Street Fair, Japantown, San Francisco

California State Horseman's American Horse Show, Sonoma

"Annie and Mary Day," Blue Lake

Santa Clara County Fair, San Jose

Indian Fair Days, Sierra Mono Museum, North Fork

Gilroy Garlic Festival

Petaluma River Festival

Wildwood Days and Peddlers' Fair, Rio Dell

Siskiyou County Fair and Paul Bunyan Jubilee

Calamari Festival, Santa Cruz

Jamestown Pioneer Days

El Dorado Days at Mt. Ranch, San Andreas

Mother Lode Fair and Loggers' Contest, Sonora

Plumas County Fair, Quincy

Pony Express Day, McKinleyville (August 22)

Children's Fairytale Birthday Week, Oakland

Air Round-Up, Red Bluff

Willow Creek Bigfoot Days

Adobe Day, Ide Adobe, Red Bluff

Del Norte County Fair, Crescent City

Gravenstein Apple Fair, Sebastopol

Lake County Fair, Lakeport

Renaissance Pleasure Faire, Novato

Ringling Brothers Circus, San Francisco/Oakland

Cirque du Soleil, San Francisco

❖❖ September

Renaissance Pleasure Faire, Novato

Sausalito Art Festival

Begonia Festival, Capitola

Monterey Jazz Festival

Mendocino County Fair and Apple Show, Boonville

A la Carte, A la Park, Golden Gate Park, San Francisco

San Francisco Art Festival

Redwood Empire Logging Festival, McKinleyville

Constitution Days, Nevada City

Vintage Festival, Hall of Flowers, Golden Gate Park, San Francisco

Festival of Viewing of the Moon, Japantown, San Francisco

California State Fair, Sacramento

Scottish Games, Santa Rosa Fairgrounds

Pleasanton Pasta Festival

Columbia Admission Day

Blue Grass Festival, Amador County Fairgrounds

Pageant of Fire Mountain, Guerneville

Vintage Car Fair, Fremont

Moon Festival with Chinese Dragon, Chinatown, San Francisco

Opera in the Park, Golden Gate Park, San Francisco

National Indian Observance Day, Crescent City

American Indian Pow Wow, Volcano

Paul Bunyan Days, Fort Bragg

Concord Jazz Festival

Indian "Big Time" Days, Amador County

Santa Cruz County Fair, Watsonville

Vintage Festival, Sonoma

LEAP sand castle contest for architects, Aquatic Park, San Francisco

San Francisco Blues Festival, Justin Herman Plaza and Fort Mason, San Francisco

KQED Ice Cream Social, San Francisco

Blessing of the Fishing Fleet, Fisherman's Wharf, San Francisco

Northcountry Fair, Arcata

Carmel Mission Fiesta

Fiesta del Pueblo, San Jose

Redwood Invitational Regatta, Big Lagoon, Humboldt County

Oktoberfest, San Mateo Fairgrounds

Oktoberfest, San Jose

Lodi Grape Festival

Fiesta Patrias, Woodland

Castroville Artichoke Festival

Walnut Festival, Walnut Creek

Worldfest, Live Oak Park, Berkeley

Sonoma Valley of the Moon Festival, Sonoma Mission State Historic Park

Sourdough Days, Sutter Hill

Weaverville Bigfoot Daze

Bridge to Bridge Run, Bay Bridge to Golden Gate Bridge, San Francisco

Grand National Livestock Exposition Rodeo & Horse Show, Cow Palace, San Francisco

❖ October

Laguna Seca Grand Prix, Monterey

Fortuna Arts Festival

Sonoma Country Harvest Festival, Santa Rosa

Fresno Fair

National Livestock Expo, Cow Palace, San Francisco

Marin Grape Festival, San Rafael

Pumpkin Festival, Half Moon Bay

Football season starts

Spanishtown Art and Pumpkin Festival

Columbia Fiddle and Banjo Contest

Candle Lighter Ghost House, Fremont

Pro-Am Surfing International, Santa Cruz

Old Mill Days, Bale Grist Mill State Historic Park

Redding Children's Art Festival

Fall Festival, Clearlake Oaks

Selma Parade and Band Festival

Johnny Appleseed Day, Paradise

Lumberjack Day, West Point

Harbor Festival, Morro Day

Great Sandcastle Building Contest, Carmel

Great Snail Race, Folsom

Oktoberfest, Tahoe City

Old Timers' Day, King City

Columbus Day Festival, San Francisco

Reedley Festival

Chinese Double Ten Celebration, San Francisco

San Francisco International Film Festival

Discovery Day, Bodega Bay

Harvest Hoedown, Healdsburg

November

North California Boat and Sports Show, Oakland

Christmas Balloon Parade, San Jose (day after Thanksgiving)

Thanksgiving Art Fair, Mendocino

December

Grandma's Christmas Open House, Anderson Marsh State Historic Park

Pioneer Christmas, Bale Grist Mill State Historic Park

Christmas at the Mission, Sonoma Mission State Historic Park

Christmas Art and Music Festival, Eureka

Great Dickens Faire, San Francisco

Nutcracker Suite, San Francisco Ballet

Nutcracker Suite, Oakland Ballet

Currier & Ives Christmas Open House, Sutter Creek

Festival of the Trees, Monterey

Festival of the Trees, San Rafael

Lighting of the Tree of Lebanon, Santa Rosa

Native Christmas Tree Ceremony, Sequoia National Park

Christmas Tree Lane, Fresno

Pioneer Christmas Party, Ide Adobe, Red Bluff

Rice-Pounding Ceremony, Japantown, San Francisco

Miner's Christmas, Columbia

Amador Calico Christmas

San Juan Bautista da Posada Fiesta

Victorian Christmas, Nevada City

Festival of Lights, Volcano

St. Nicolas in the Barnyard, Carmel Valley

New Year's Eve Fireman's Ball, Cloverdale

Claim Jumper's New Year's Eve Square Dance, Plymouth

INDEX